For Nelda
With lov
wishes, &
own joy...

Coralie R

MW01265304

THE JOURNEY WITHIN:
Living After Loss

CORALIE HARLOW ROBERTSON

Betterfly Press

ISBN 978-1-927730-07-2
First edition
Published by Betterfly Press
Layout & Design by Robyn York / Portage Publishing

ACKNOWLEDGMENTS

This book would not have been possible without the willing contributions of the 50 people I interviewed. Their stories were inspiring and will facilitate healing in readers who have experienced similar losses. Telling their stories was painful at times, so I am very grateful they chose to speak publicly even though their names and identifying places have been changed. I am humbled by the trust they showed in me by granting permission to use their stories of loss and rebuilding their lives. The treasure trove of material gained from their sharing in depth is the heart and soul of this book.

My profound thanks go to my mentor, friend, and encourager, Ed White. Thank you for the legions of wisdom-filled sessions. I am blessed by your unending support, faith in me, and willingness to edit during the long writing and interviewing process. I could never have written this without you. You helped me to believe I could write a book. You let me go so I could spread my wings, but I always knew you were there, one email away.

I want to thank my daughter, Marianne, for her loving support and technical help. Her willingness to give of her time and expertise proved very valuable.

The following professionals gave me permission to use their names as recognized experts in their fields:

Dave Helms Ph.D. Psychotherapist, Austin, Texas

John Hudak, Director, Community Counseling Center, Cape Girardeau, Missouri

Bradley Robison M.D. Founder, Sacred Space, Cape Girardeau, Missouri

Perry Sanderford Ph.D. Founder, Crossroads Counseling Center, Brandon, Mississippi

Grace Harlow Klein Ph.D., Psychotherapist, Center for Human Encouragement, Rochester, New York

My sister, Grace Harlow Klein, also partnered with me in ways for which I will always be grateful. Grace is an outstanding writer of several books on loss. I am honored she shared her insights in the chapter, "Loss and Grief." I'm not sure which has supported me more: her belief in me as my sister, or her skills as a psychotherapist guiding me through my own relationship experience. Additionally, Grace served as my editor, making everything in these pages better.

Table of Contents

Preface

Following the death of my husband of 54 years, I became independent for the first time in my adult life. When I met Will, I was not looking for a relationship, but we did have scintillating conversations. One day, on a lark, Will,, my friend and mentor, suggested that we interview our friends asking what qualities attract you when out with a member of the opposite sex? I soon experienced, for the first time, that this informal questioning elicited answers that piqued my interest. I liked the feeling of being connected to people's lives. People opened up to me. I decided to go further. When I landed my first interview, Will presented me with a gift of my trusty recorder that I have used in 50 subsequent interviews.

As I talked with people, I began to experience a path that was to become familiar. As I interviewed someone, they suggested others to interview. The first person I interviewed was John Hudak, Director of Community Counseling Center in my hometown of Cape Girardeau, Missouri. He was clear that it is not going to work for long to fill the loneliness and grief void with another person. I was to hear variations of this theme from other professionals.

My sister, Grace Harlow Klein, led me to many people when I asked her. I needed diversity of location and people to interview in other parts of the country. I still believed, at this point that a new relationship was the way to go to stem grief, but I let the interviews lead me as a pattern developed.

What I got from the 50 people I ultimately interviewed was that it didn't work that way. That's when the working title began to change. Originally Will and I called our book project *Free to be Playmates Forever*. *The Journey Within* came to me about midway through the process. I began to travel. I talked to people I wouldn't have normally talked to, because I was, by now, hungry to hear more experiences.

I started out with a long list of possible interview questions. I discovered I was often cutting off the flow by changing a line of questioning. I learned to listen more carefully to what they were saying and build on the next question from there. I was a rookie interviewer, excited by my own journey. I have changed all identifying information and names except for the recognized experts who agreed to my naming them. I have also used real names in the story of Nancy Sharp. She is the author of Both Sides Now, her personal story of transformation.

The stories led me to name the chapters and focus on the issues I learned as I progressed. The interviews turned out to be the easy part. Recorded, they had to be transcribed by hand and then typed to have documents to work with that would be accurate to each person's story. Unless they deferred the offer, I sent the finished document to each person to review. They were free to correct information or to add comments so that the documents reflected a level of comfort with their story.

Many of the people I interviewed were inspired to change or modify what I sent them in the first draft of their story. Only one woman who had been very open with her experiences called me to say she had second thoughts about her children's reaction to reading her candid story.

I offered to withdraw her story if it were her wishes, thanking her for the experience of interviewing her.

Reading the first draft sometimes stimulated memory resulting in the respondent's desire to include new things not covered in the first draft. Or they chose to redact or revise certain parts. I welcomed this process. I encouraged additional input or revisions. In the end, the revisions produced positive results.

All direct comments from each person's story are in quotes.

For myself, I didn't want to accept that Will was my transitional relationship, but that became apparent in time. Acceptance became a theme in my own relationship journey.

CHAPTER 1
Free As You'll Ever Be

Then one day it happens to us…loss, mind-numbing loss, whether due to death or a failed relationship. We are alone. It is a scared space we occupy for a long time. Someone reaches out to us saying, "I can help." A relationship begins. Here's how it was for me…

The Coralie and Will Story

It might as well have been spring. Three years after my husband of 54 years passed away, I came alive again. Married very young, I had had little or no dating experience.

Fiercely independent and self-aware, I thought my life was complete with a strong and attentive family and many friends. Then I met Will. I didn't learn until much later that he was actually 14 years older than me. He didn't look it or act it. A widower for six years, he had all the qualities that were not only attractive to me, but also even desirable. He was intelligent, successful, and a good conversationalist. Above all, he was articulate. I fell in love with his words. Words are important to me. They bring me life and satisfaction.

My son observed that I was acting like a twit, giggling and breathless. I reminded him I was my own person and not bound by what other people thought. I couldn't stop smiling. Before long we were zipping about the countryside safely ensconced in his Cadillac SRX. The chemistry was there. My brain was soon bathed in an Oxytocin high. We could talk for hours.

Of course, just like many transitional relationships, eventually reality hit, and life issues crashed the party boat

I was on. I learned I was dealing with a very complex man with commitment issues.

I think our souls may be connected. We both have grown. During the journey, I found the courage to be vulnerable and the willingness to risk. I trust the process. The final chapter has not yet been written.

Whether my own relationship story will turn out to be a transitional one or metamorphosis into a lasting, solid, intimate friendship is not yet known. What keeps me from giving up is exuberance, curiosity, and above all, hope.

One common element in stories of people rebuilding their lives after loss is struggle. Most often, true growth is accompanied by a lot of struggle. The journey involves waking up whole segments of ourselves. After loss, we need to remember that time does not heal all wounds, it is the process within that heals the wounds, leaving us free to choose the next chapter of our lives-new relationships, even failures, but taking the risk to live again. The first informants are Andre and Cera, whose early relationships were characterized by struggle. Then they met.

The Andre and Cera Story

Andre and Cera's story shows that experience is the roadmap. If we learn from our failed experiences, we can arrive at another place in a new relationship. Andre tells that his 25-year first marriage produced four children and was problematical almost from the beginning. "There were three separations and reconciliations. We had third party counseling. When the divorce finally came, I realized there was no way for the marriage to continue.

It was a mutual decision, but it was more she than I. We agreed we should stop trying."

Children turned out to be a major stress on the relationship. The four children were born with difficulty. "Our first child was born in the fourth year of our marriage. Three and one-half years later, the twins were born. Then two and one-half years later, our fourth child was born. They needed so much from us, and neither of us was in a position to provide it. We were mutually parenting during the separations. There were actually three separations. When the divorce settled years later, two of the children were out of the home; one went with her and one with me."

Cera, on the other hand, was married a lot later. She was 36 at the time. Her father was abusive to her sexually, but supported her in other ways, so she was conflicted. She remembers. "I did not want to be close to anybody. I escaped, eventually, because my husband was alcoholic. I didn't know what I was getting into. I stayed married 12 years because my background said once you made a commitment, you should stick with it. I realized that wasn't going to work so I made a decision"

"Finally, we separated. I didn't want anything from him. I didn't want to be a parasite or be dependent. I did learn about standing on my own two feet in the presence of someone who was very difficult. We went through a series of discussions. I would write up notes. In some ways, we learned something through conversations about what went wrong between us." Cera recalls that she was 48 by the time they divorced.

Andre describes relationships he had before he met
Cera. "I had two relationships, but I never married. One
relationship person wanted to marry, but I didn't. We
parted by mutual arrangement. There was no rancor. There
was sadness. What she wanted and what I wanted were
different. Another one lasted several years and ended with
much rancor and personal violence. I learned a lot from
my relationships.

I was 61 by then in '92."

Cera said one thing she loved about Andre was that he
wasn't dependent. "I wasn't going to be the whole thing
he hung onto. That was very important to me. Together we
achieved our place with ourselves and our careers."

Cera continues, "It helped me to grow and develop as
a person. That was attractive to me. I felt comfortable."
Andre and Cera often continue each other's thoughts.
Andre added, "You call this work. It was. I was in analysis
for years. Cera was also in therapy. We look at ourselves
and grow. We have no choice. From the beginning I
looked at this woman and noticed she has magic. I saw
that. People who know her adore her or at least are happy
to be with her. She is a joy to be around. I like common
English words to describe her: beautiful, enthusiastic.
Her approach to every situation is, 'I'll try it. Let's do
something different.' Yes! She's a yes person. She has an
affirmation toward life. Run with it! Do it!"

Cera captures their relationship, "I loved Andre's
thoughtful qualities. He was fascinated by ideas. We could
talk for hours, delving into things. I felt that right away.
I was coming out on the other side of what I had been
through. Andre knew of that process. I felt understood.

There was tremendous attraction between us, which was odd because there had been no attraction with my first husband. It was a way for me to escape. He thought my father was going to help him with his business."

Cera has written a book about successful aging. Her insights always are apparent. She asks, "What do we do about it now that Andre and I are together? This is one of the positive things about life and aging. Something bad happens to you early in life. You find a way to get through it. The message is, "I coped then. I will cope now." Nothing is going to tear me to shreds. I'm not going to let that happen. There is a way to cope with everything. I can say I'm grateful, not for what happened, but what I learned. It's what serves me for the rest of my life."

Cera and Andre enjoy beauty in all its forms. They visited a state park. There were waterfalls, woods, and pathways. They felt they could stay there for hours. Their mutual love of good music is apparent. Cera recalls, "I was a musician. Andre was a singer. He sang the bass part in Handel's Messiah. How joyful to be in the middle of that rather than outside it. We had feelings of mutuality in things. He liked my sculpture. It was odd, so contemporary. We connected."

Andre has some thoughts on the success of relationship. "I was drawn to her right away. I couldn't stop thinking about her. There was a thunderbolt of chemistry. If there isn't, don't try to make it there because if it is, it will survive all kinds of things. There is no substitute. You must also have great conversations. In the morning, when there is no need to jump out of bed, we make up spontaneous stories. We have fun doing it. We enjoy what's going on between us. What I think relationships need to be good is kindness. Without trust and kindness, don't bother to continue a relationship. Also common interests and ideas are vital. Kindness manifests itself in please and thank you. Treat each other with respect. This is another human being."

Andre observes, "We're so solid in our relationship, it rubs off on people. People feel good with us. We are able to give others so much because we have what we need. So we get people to do great things for us. Having your own stuff in order is essential to relationships. My first relationship was predicated on the idea that she was needy, and I was going to rescue her. One rescuer and one needy person won't work. You give, take and share."

Andre feels most of their challenges have come through the circumstance that Cera had to accept his four children. The four children plus two grandchildren had already been brought into the world. Cera was successful with the position, "You don't have to love me, and I don't have to love you. We'll just see what happens. It worked out great."

Andre and Cera are trying to make the most out of every day. They both have a deep and abiding love of beauty, music, sculpture, poetry, and the out-of-doors. They set the clock most days so they can cuddle. They exchange a lot of notes, a lot of "I love you's." Every summer, they go to Maine. The tide, the ocean - they hear the surf. They fall asleep listening to that simplicity.

The theme of struggle is apparent in the story of Andre and Cera. Cera, as well, experienced pain and struggle during her first marriage that lasted 12 years. Can there be something that occurs during struggle that supports growth? They both evolved. Andre and Cera's story gives us hope. What keeps us going is not what has been taken from us, but what we have yet to give and who we have yet to become.

CHAPTER 2
One is a Lonely Word

Wake up. Our world is changing. Many relationships fail. If through death or the end of a relationship you have suffered the loss of a spouse or partner, you are going to be lonely at times. Loneliness is a particularly relevant issue to spouses who are trying to live again. Their rates of mortality, illness, and depression exceed those of their married counterparts. After much research and many interviews with recognized experts and people from all walks of life, one thing becomes clear. Defending against loneliness is no way to establish a relationship with a person of the opposite sex. According to psychotherapist and Community Counseling Center Director, John Hudak, "Why would you think someone else could do what you're not willing to do yourself?" You have to deal with your own loneliness.

For those who have not had the experience, it is impossible to understand the depth of the pain caused by the loss of a mate, either by death or divorce. Those hurting gradually need to regain a taste for life. Can dating help? Looking at dating stories, successful or struggling, can become a source of inspiration and hope for others. Modeling strategies for living will promote persons who have suffered loss to move on with their lives. The other choice is being cut off from reality and sinking into isolation. Whether you succumb to loneliness and give up or bounce back to become a stronger person is up to you.

According to Dave Helms an Austin, Texas psychotherapist, there needs to be new rules with an aging population. Most of the rules in the old model stop at age 65. The average lifespan is now 84 and increasing every year. What are you going to do not only concerning work, but socially, health wise and spiritually for 20 years or more? We're going to have to respond to aging differently in the future. There could very well be several serial relationships.

Dating After Loss

Say you are a vital woman who marries again after the loss of a husband. Your second husband dies. You are a vital woman who is still reasonably healthy. How will we view a possible third relationship? It can be wildly complex. Now we have four generations of blended families. How we're going about it accounts for some of the struggles in the relationships of seniors.

One factor that all people who live alone have in common is that sooner or later, they are lonely. According to John Cacioppo, Director of the Center for Cognitive and Social Neuroscience at the University of Chicago, people who feel consistently lonely have a 14% higher risk of premature death than those who don't. Cacioppo says, "Loneliness is a risk factor for early death beyond what can be explained by poor health behaviors." (Hellmich)

The theme of loneliness is central to dating after loss. Can a person really die of a broken heart? "It's very real," said Dr. Scott Sharkey, a cardiologist with the Minneapolis Heart Institute. Researchers found that widows and widowers had a 30% elevated risk of death in the first six months after their spouse had died.

John Hudak took issue with the wisdom of focusing on dying at any stage of our life. He noted when people get into the "before I die..." mode, there is a disconnect with what goes on right now. People need to be engaged. When you disengage, you lose ground.

Hudak felt, "If dating can support people achieving their human potential when they come to counseling following loss, they need to be encouraged to do so. If they can begin to believe 'maybe this time...', they develop a mindset that there is more for them to be, so many other things are possible. They need to be supported to ask, 'what does it mean to be firing on all my pistons?'"

Being lonely may be very painful when the essence of who your spouse was is gone due to Alzheimer's or other forms of dementia. Choosing to date while the spouse is still living can become a controversial moral issue. John Hudak, is very compassionate.

"The need to connect is a universal issue, not just a dating issue." In his opinion, if the essence of a spouse is gone, the relationship may be broken." Even though that choice to date may flout a carefully held belief, dating while the spouse is still living, may be the alternative to dying."

In exploring loneliness following the loss of a spouse, the question inevitably comes up, what happens to those who choose not to date? Elaine is such a woman:

The Elaine Story

"My husband and I met at church. Back when I was a teenager, I prayed that God would send to me the person he wanted me to marry. Bob and I met at church, and I never really dated anyone else. We had very similar interests. We just fell in love and were married 54 years before he passed away."

Elaine didn't think it was disrespectful to her late husband
to date someone else. She explained, "If God really sends
someone to my door and tells me I want you to date this
guy, then I would consider it, but I don't feel the need to
date. I am comfortable in my own skin. I am busy. I don't
feel I need to hang onto a guy to make me complete. I
am active in several things at my church. I have a lot of
friends. I have family. Just get out of yourself and focus
on others. When you're focused on yourself is when you
could have a little pity party. Just look around. There are
people all around us who need help, need encouragement.
Just do that."

How do we define loneliness? Loneliness means to be cut
off from others. It can involve the sadness of being alone,
grief, or a condition of bleakness. In short, it is painful.
Can it be measured? What makes us vulnerable to making
unsuitable choices?

Of the many people we interviewed, perhaps the one
who best exemplifies the power of the word loneliness is
Danielle. Her story suggests the ways in which loneliness
can be ameliorated.

The Danielle Story

Danielle had been lonely even before her husband of
nearly 50 years passed away. When her late husband
slipped into heart disease, he gradually pulled away from
her and spent a lot of his time under a proverbial rock,
feeling ill. Danielle experienced loneliness long before
her husband left her. Taking care of him became isolating,
so she gradually began to seek friends and activities to
compensate. Golf became her game. When her husband

died, she assumed she would cope fairly well because she was somewhat accustomed to being alone.

He passed. Now she was completely alone. It was somewhat disconcerting to her when she began to experience physical illness in various parts of her body. "Why now?", she asked herself. Her body felt her loneliness and responded with illness.

To her illness, Danielle added some depression. One day she was playing with her golfing friends in a competition. She could barely make it through the first nine holes. She informed her golfing partner she was unable to go on. She thought her partner would understand because she herself was a widow. To her chagrin, her friend began to lecture her on staying the course. Near tears, as she was making her way to the clubhouse, she ran into an old friend, a man she had known since high school. He asked her why she was quitting the course, and she found herself releasing the story about how misunderstood she felt.

They ended up going to dinner, and she experienced that, indeed, she didn't feel so alone. It felt good to connect with someone. He was a widower, and could talk, vulnerably about his grief. It's good to talk with someone who's gone through similar loss. Having been lonely for several years before her husband died, it helped to connect with someone who had also experienced loneliness.

Loneliness sometimes involves fear. Many women, especially those who have been caretakers in their previous relationship, have fears of becoming too attached in the next relationship. They don't want to have the next significant other die on them. Many are looking for a guy just to hang out with, but most seem to want just one thing, sexual intimacy. A typical woman may ask, "Am I doomed to loneliness for the rest of my days?" Charity projects and thinking of others don't always fill loneliness. You can be lonely in a crowd.

One of my good friends, Anna, observed that after several years of loneliness, she now was ready to be strong enough to share her life with another,but she wasn't in any hurry. Until she could find that right person, she was comfortable being alone.

The Anna Story

She enrolled in an adult education course in her local community college. The professor was personable, and soon they were having coffee together. Her loneliness was abating. After some time, difficulties arose. Before he could know her as a person, it became apparent that Randall was interested in sex. Anna considered this to be a red flag.

"Men are very visual," she lamented. Anna continues, "It presents problems to be attracted to someone who is visual. I have to be engaged in keeping the wall up. He's focused on trying to scale it. A lot of my life, I've been attractive to men. I want him to see the 'me' that is inside. I want him to shut his eyes. Forget what I look like. I live inside what's attractive. That's not all there is. There is a person here. A personality. Thoughts. Feelings. I would like for him to listen to me. See how I use my self-discipline for my health, food intake, and behavior. He thinks he's the only man who has given me attention. He is not. If he cannot appreciate the whole person I am, I could just move on."

Anna could be tempted to conclude that because this romantic relationship fell apart, she will fail in all other relationships. In truth, she has fallen back into loneliness, thinking all future tries might be similarly doomed. Many retreat back into solitude. Granted, finding that love can be much harder than when you were younger. There are not as many single people as when you were in college.

Regardless of how resourceful we are there will be times when our efforts to lesson loneliness will fail. Women are sometimes vulnerable to the danger of premature sexual intimacy as a method of relieving loneliness.

On occasion people enter into relationships too quickly. It would be beneficial to take some time to consider a couple of questions. What is it you really want? What would you like to have happen? We need to believe we have the flexibility to weather any storm gracefully. Emotions can be scary. Why are you letting it stop you? Nothing guarantees you're not going to be lonely. You can engage with other people. Step out and find people who need a friend.

John Hudak has indicated that loneliness is one of the most physically and emotionally debilitating experiences humans can suffer. "To avoid illness and even death if it goes on too long, his advice is to stay with it, see what it has to say. Dying of a broken heart can become a reality if we run from it, if we just want it to go away."

Solitude

Hudak differentiates between loneliness and solitude. "Solitude is a good place to be if you spend time looking at the holes in your existence. See what they have to tell you.

Pay attention to pain. We are not a society that pays attention to where it hurts. Metaphorically, we take an aspirin to make it go away instead of going through it. We need to embrace being alone, get focused, and become centered. If we don't deal with it, it's going to make it worse."

Pain and difficulty can sometimes serve as a pathway to a new level of involvement. According to Hudak, you can change your world if you stay with it, see what it has to say. One of the traits of a resilient person is taking personal responsibility for whatever emotions we're feeling. Hudak says, "We must start with ourselves. Anytime we look to other people to fill a void within ourselves, we're going to be disappointed. It's not going to happen, no matter what. We need to feel what loneliness is. Don't expect others to do it for us. What we're feeling may be emptiness, anxiety, disconnection, or separation from others. These are all pieces that go into what loneliness is."

Considering the universal need to connect, Hudak says people can find ways to do that other than dating. He notes work can be a satisfaction, as well as volunteering, grandkids, hobbies, anything wherein people can lose themselves in something.

The Annette Story

Annette had some thoughts on loneliness when I interviewed her. She believes loneliness is a choice. She noted we all have a lot of options: coffee, lunch, church, volunteering, and helping others. She grants that she sometimes begins to feel lonelier if she is down physically. By herself, she will feel more fragile. She maintains, if you're lonely all the time, it's a choice.

Annette says, "There can be an emotional danger of being lonely. I sometimes miss the company of men. Men are different; their perspective is different. There is some longing to be part of a couple. The world is designed around couples. Yes, I think it would be nice to be part of a couple."

Annette thinks we are vulnerable after loss no matter how long it has been. She notes she had been divorced four years, but she hadn't done all of the work in her inner self when she started dating Bryan. She says, "I trusted him not knowing he had ulterior issues. I was probably looking for companionship. At that point, yes, I was lonely. I missed male company."

The most important advice Annette had to give a woman who has suffered loss and was perhaps feeling lonely pointed to the inner self: "Before you can have a relationship, you have to know yourself. You can't know who you are until you come to know why you are. You will never get back to where or who you were before you suffered loss. You are forever changed. Time must go by. But, you can come out of the shadows of loss and be more self-aware, more aware of the world around you and better prepared for a new relationship. There must be someone out there who will care for who you are. I didn't know who I was after my losses. Don't go forward until you are secure and grounded enough to have a good relationship."

Dave Helms, Austin, Texas, psychotherapist, notes that the biggest danger from extended loneliness is, of course, suicide. Research shows loneliness is also a risk factor for early death. Helms says, "The biggest difference between loneliness and solitude or aloneness depends on whether the person affected can view the self openly. Viewing the self as lonely creates a false image of oneself. If they begin to have thoughts like 'I caused it', they may view themselves as ill. Continued thoughts like that may indeed produce a negative result in a variety of ways."

"They may start looking into anything to fill the aloneness void. They may internalize 'who am I as an individual?' If the sufferer looks to another person to fill the void, the relationship with the next person they relate to and start to depend on won't work. Eventually, anger will come out in some form. This can be accompanied by lack of trust, lack of significance, loss of power when the person covers up loss with another person. What the wounded person brings with them is some sensitivity to covering the void with another. A lot depends on how powerless they're feeling. But this 'too soon' relationship is not going to work."

Helms also notes that when you lose a spouse, your world changes. Your grieving may cause you to have difficulty thinking and making decisions. One of the dangers of loneliness after loss is that it could create irrational behavior. For example, you could be prone to contracting every illness that comes along, at least in your mind.

Helms has his take on what qualities are required to have positive relationships. Especially as it concerns older people looking for a companion, he maintains, "A large part of life meaning has come from what we have accomplished and shared experiences. As we get older, the principal element of satisfaction comes from character, not experiences. The challenge is how to prepare for the vital need for continued character development. We are looking for moral excellence and firmness. We need strong mental and ethical traits, notable, conspicuous traits. The other choice is bitterness, fear, and self-serving qualities. They used to call these character disorders; now they call them spectrum disorders. Whatever you call them, they don't make for satisfaction in lives. It is strong character that underlies positive relationships."

Dr. Bradley D. Robison, M.D., psychiatrist and Director of an organization called Sacred Space, believes psychology and spirituality overlap when dealing with loneliness and loss. He says you have to understand the complexity of what's going on. He points out that relieving loneliness with family, friends, and activities would differ from lifting loneliness through connecting with members of the opposite sex. Dr. Robison says, "There are different types of intimacy, different layers of intimacy. When I think of spiritual or existential intimacy, I'm not just thinking of relationship, but a deeper sense of connection around a deeper core. The significance of an existential sense of connection is what I call Sacred Space. Sacred Space is when you have intimacy that is a shared awareness that you are in the presence of God. With various people, when you speak of loneliness, you're really talking about various levels or kinds of intimacy. Each individual is different in their need for different kinds of intimacy."

Dr. Robison feels one has to turn inside for a lessening of loneliness. He maintains there are many people who misinterpret scripture that two people should become one. This leads to an unhealthy type of intimacy. He says, "I use a metaphor of ships, a perception in our culture that two ships become one by tying themselves off to one another. Particularly if you're in the early part if a relationship, like two ships, you come together in a calm, quiet atmosphere, and it feels very good. But ultimately, with all this connection, and when you get out of this safe, quiet harbor and into life, it doesn't work. Two ships can't sail across the ocean if they're tied together. It creates a false picture of intimacy. Each ship has to attend themselves, be responsible, and have boundaries. It depends on whether you're being responsible TO or responsible FOR someone you're intimate with."

If you move too quickly after loss, there's not a right/wrong timeline, but there is definitely a right or wrong approach in the healing of the heart. If you're looking to someone else to bolster parts of the heart you can't do on your own, it's as if you're tying your ship to a more powerful ship that is going to be able to carry you through. Unfortunately, people are willing to let that happen. Again, it feels great at first. Dr. Robison notes, "You have to be a whole individual. Your ship has to be healthy. You have to be truly ready for a journey before you can develop true intimacy that really allows for the uniqueness of the individual."

Robison says, "I see elements of that present in individuals who move too quickly back into relationship because they're not allowing themselves an opportunity to heal fully. When you talk about intimacy or loneliness, you can't go too far down that path before you're talking about identity. Ultimately, the longing of the heart is for validation. Validation can be healthy or unhealthy. True intimacy is about the deeper elements of myself I didn't even know, as I support another's understanding of who I am.

CHAPTER 3
Drop Off Your Baggage

By the time a person reaches middle age, it is safe to say he or she will have baggage of one sort or another. Herein, the focus will be on a person who may screw up a potential relationship because they can't let go of something.

Perry Sanderford, Ph.D. whose doctorate is in philosophy, psychology, and counseling and is the founder of Crossroads Counseling Center in Brandon, Mississippi, says seniors bring baggage to relationships because life brings pain and people bring struggle to relationship. When seniors attempt a relationship, they bring trauma. "It's the past invading the present and bringing it into the future."

Dr. Sanderford observes, "We put on the other person the responsibility of fixing us. I think of it as a container, and if they are the container, some of them come with more ability. The responsibility for fixing us is not healthy if you're expecting the other to fill up your container."

Dr. Sanderford thinks that learning how to build healthy relationships could help people let go of their baggage. "One of the secrets to having healthy relationships is to come to the relationship not for what I can get out of it, but what I bring to it. The lesson is not selfishness, but selflessness. Intimacy grows from serving one another in that safe secure place where both people have a voice and bring something to the relationship for the other person. That creates a sense of intimacy. Some people like that idea, but actually bring to the relationship more of a sense that's it's really better to receive than give."

There may be baggage hidden in the disinclination of a person to pursue a new relationship following loss. Such was the case with Victor even five years after the tragic loss of his wife, Lynn, who died at only 48 years of age with esophageal cancer. He agrees that he hasn't yet reached closure over the loss of Lynn. Victor says "she was my only true love and was my soul mate. I feel I had the love of my life and am not sure I could find another or want to."

Dr. Sanderford suggests that when a person has suffered such a loss as Victor's, they might learn to live healthy again and develop healthy relationships by starting with other types of relationships. Getting rid of baggage often involves the very great value of having close friends to share your life with. If you share the joy of living and loving with a close friend, you develop a standard of love, first with self, then with God, then with friends and community. If you do all that, you don't put such a great strain on a single relationship to meet all your needs.

The Victor Story

If you don't take steps to build healthy relationships, people sometimes become bitter after loss. Victor actually went through a period of time where he was mad at God for taking his wife. He went through much soul searching.

Soul searching about forming a new relationship may also suggest a different kind of baggage: legacy issues. Victor is twelve years older than his wife, Lynn. Victor never really thought about having to save money due to their age difference but just thought basically as the patriarch of the family that he needed to support them while living and after death. He never really thought about the age difference especially when they were married and had kids as they were still both young. As it turns out he only needed to make sure they were financially sound during their living lives as she passed first. He thinks another reason he is not out looking for another mate is that he wants his savings to go to his kids not another woman. He knows that can be taken care of legally if he finds someone else, but how do you tell someone (and not affect the relationship) that all his money when he dies goes to his kids.

Merging history and resources can create great difficulties. Sanderford says most men do have legacy issues when it comes to a new relationship. There are major decisions to be made. It can feel like a sense of betrayal to adult children. They see change coming, and if the family resources are put at risk for another family that has no ties, there can be a sense of betrayal, which can bring fears that they could experience loss of what they might have inherited. It should flow to the children. If it flows in the direction of others who have not had a part in that, then that is a problem.

The new woman might feel that you're not leaving room for us to do well, and if something happened, I would get nothing. A compromise could be saying everything acquired to this point flows to the children, but from this point on, the new person could share in the things we acquire together. Old resources flow back to my children, but from this point on, it is possible to make that division so the new person can benefit also while still protecting the children.

As Dr. Perry Sanderford has observed, learning how to build healthy relationships could help people let go of their baggage. Such is the case with Greg who has never been married despite many relationships. He has commitment issues, but hopes that his experiences have produced a willingness to let go of his commitment baggage.

The Greg Story

"This is how it would go early on with my forays into relationship. I was reluctant to go out with friends. My last relationship failure had made me wary. It was Christmas time two years ago. We go out. It was a cozy place, families out for Christmas. I see her; she sees me; we make eye contact; I never intended to go talk to her. After having drinks, I gave her my number and left.

I was attracted to her physically. She had a bright smile, pretty curly hair beaming toward me. She got the hook in me. She liked to ski. We both enjoyed outdoor, physical activities. It went well until it didn't. Things went downhill. She was unstable mentally. An example was the illusions she had about our relationship. I thought because we were attracted, I could give her the benefit of the doubt. It ended up being a bad mess.

Why couldn't I see what was coming earlier? Because I am a romantic, this is more of my baggage. Early on, I was a hopeless romantic. I was the Marrying Sam type. I had a dream of a career, children, and a big house. I wanted a big life. As time went on through several relationships, the dream slowly eroded. Who I wanted to be was NOT who I was. I slowly chipped away at the veneer of what I thought happiness should be. My own illusions chipped away. Finally it really cracked through that I wasn't the Marrying Sam type. As I met different women ranging from disturbed to healthy, I began to realize it wasn't them, it was me."

What followed were profound insights into Greg's self-awareness. "When I met a girl and our relationship progressed according to her timeline, inevitably, things would start to deteriorate. Instead of a mature look at what was happening, I would blame the woman. It ended up at a point where I changed. I found out this isn't what I want. The baggage was that I was trying to put square pegs into round holes. Thinking it's them but admitting it's me was hard. I would latch onto an idea and insert a feeling that wasn't me so in time the feeling went away, and I let go of the idea. These women wanted marriage and babies."

Greg began to acknowledge a pattern in his relationships: "I would fall in love with the next one. It would fail. I would recognize this isn't you. Bounce back and do it again. When things fell apart, the relationship failed. I would eat crow, go home, and hang on by my fingernails. I let go and started playing the guitar. To relieve my feelings of numbness, I started studying the classical guitar. I stayed home, killed the current relationship and played the guitar 24-7 trying to hold onto something inside. I stayed with nurturing this feeling. You can't survive lying to yourself. I got better. Like anything being born, it hurts. I finally took on a new sense of self. After that, relationships were different. I let go of things easier. There was less pain than in the past."

Greg turned to different activities in his life. He began riding motorcycles, bicycles, and playing the guitar. He ended up in the Boston Conservatory of Music. It took complete commitment, no outside relationships. What he didn't like was being sedentary long enough to go professional with his music. "I took to racing bikes and getting back to honesty. What I thought would make me happy in my activities turned out not to be. It was a change in the right direction. When you nurture that which really serves you, if you're lucky, you can let go of what does not."

One of the insights Greg observed is that people get caught up in patterns of the type of people they are attracted to. "What I discovered is when you're not whole, you'll find people who will abuse you. In Boston, I found Beth. She was someone who was well educated, but a recovering alcoholic, but you'd never know it in a million years. She was three months sober when I started dating her. What came crashing down is that as wonderful as soberness is, often they can't handle themselves without alcohol. Once again, I brought baggage. I abandoned her. I had thought I could handle it. She would have a panic attack, break down and have hysterics. I thought my love would cure her. At her worst, she punched me across the face."

One of the things Greg learned about himself is that he over estimates his staying power. They began looking at real estate together. She came from money. "We stayed at Martha's Vineyard for the summer. I realized I couldn't afford this. There was no way out of this. I decided I couldn't do this. I broke it off. I got a big slap across the face. Once again, I had good intentions, but ended up with a bad, hurting result because I lied to her. I did not understand what alcoholism is. That doesn't change. They deal with it better. It took me a while to get over what an SOB I was.

So Greg refocused his life. He began to slowly get in touch with who he really is and become a more authentic person. He believes asking the right questions of yourself is where it starts. "You have to know what you want. Where am I with bike racing and the guitar? How can I improve? What are my limiters? Once I realized I couldn't stand not feeling a sense of progression, I knew I was on the right track. Dating would affect schoolwork. I was sick of spinning my wheels with relationships. I need to do something that feels good and see it through."

Greg knew he was on a good path with the bicycle. He got his racing license. He acknowledges, "I never honored that. Relationships got in the way. I would let everything go for the relationship. There came a time when I began to see a woman I met at work on weekends. That's all. It stays right there. I am happy with that. Enjoy it as it is for now. There is no problem. I don't push for more. She doesn't need me emotionally. It's nice for me. Still, there's that unrealistic void. I want someone to fill it. Watch out! If you were to get what you think you want in a relationship it might not work. My thinking is that I've got time; she's got time. No agenda. Take a step out. Let the progression happen. Turn up the volume very slowly. Let go of control. Let little things add up. Have faith."

The Will Story

Evidences of baggage can readily be found in most people of a "certain age." Whether my interview with Will indicated baggage or merely a strong, complex character is unclear. In either case, his is an interesting story. He has never adjusted to being by himself following the long illness and death of his wife. He was only partly joking when he remarked, "I would have dated the devil herself had she been available."

Will believes he's still involved in the process of grieving the loss of the love of his life at some level. "I think of her every day. Possibly, it is a barrier to ever committing myself to anyone else. Still, maybe I do feel a more mature ability to look at things with clearer perspective. The emotional state of being deprived with my wife's illness caused me to be numb for a long time.

I believe I'm beginning to emerge from that. I think what comes with age is the increasing ability to separate what's important from what's unimportant. The emotional state improves and you are able to judge things without the emotion that was present when you were younger. "

Will muses that unfortunately, "I may look at things with less enthusiasm. I was in very bad shape following my long years of caregiving when my wife died. I was physically exhausted, emotionally numb, and unfeeling to some extent, almost certainly taking everything day by day without planning for the future. The nurses' consensus at the health center, was I would not survive her death by more than three months because I was physically and emotionally exhausted. It showed. I didn't feel that far gone, and certainly, there was no release when she died anyway. It was inevitable. I had known it for years. It was just another day after day for a long time. "

Of course, Will was changed by the experience. "I wanted someone to know ME, because of all the years I'd spent with the love of my life not knowing who I was. Dementia erased all memories of our marriage, all memories of our children, and all memories of our life together. It was a blank for her. I felt like part of my life had been taken away and created a void that I wanted filled."

Of course, you can't get all those years back, ever, but Will doesn't feel resentful. He reflects, "It's useless to feel like that. You live a life; you take what happens to you. It does relate, however, to conversations I've had over the years with people my age. After ten years of depression and four years of war we came home focused on opportunity, which had been submerged in survival during those years. When we came home opportunity was there and we seized it. This concentration on making the most of what had been out of reach enabled us to achieve the greatest growth and prosperity the world has ever seen, and the fairest society we had ever had.

Central to this was the GI Bill that made higher education achievable for millions of men and women who could not otherwise have afforded it. That legislation was the greatest thing for our country since the Revolution.

Now the Greatest Generation is saddened by what we see in our society today…the disappearance of civility, loss of enthusiasm for achievement, concentration on self instead of service to others and the plunge into technology at the expense of social development. Of course not everyone is afflicted but we see so much of it.

Will began to look back at his healing process. The first person Will came in contact with was a lovely woman named Kathryn. She reached out a hand to him and said, "I can help you." But her daughter from a former marriage came first in her life. Will remembers, "I could only manage a very loose orbit round her. I could only walk on the periphery of her life. I don't think it hurt me so much as I wished it could have been another way. I learned rather quickly on the front end of our relationship, that's the way it was going to be. It never changed. We have all kinds of relationships. You can have a friendship with a person for life. But, after the loss of a spouse, it's a different relationship, different from anything I've been involved with. And a relationship is a living, breathing dynamic thing. It must grow, grow in mutual respect, mutual caring. It doesn't always have to grow into an intimate, sexual relationship, but it has to grow. When it stops growing, it goes backwards. It dies. That was what happened there. There was only so far that relationship was going to go. "

At times, there seems to be a guarded, self-protective aura about Will. He seems hesitant to go forward with a really close relationship. When asked about this, he says, "It's the way I feel. Having been so close to my wife and then losing her, I've never met any widow or widower who is anxious to repeat the experience. Most report when they did find someone, married again, and lost them, it was equally as bad as the first time around. That may be part of it, but I didn't spend a lot of time probing my inner thoughts."

Will doesn't feel being in constant pain with spinal stenosis, arthritis and other spinal issues have translated into baggage. He explains, "Only to the extent it limits me physically sometimes. You deal with it, and you go on. Obstacles in life stop where the obstacle occurs, or you go under it or around it. You can choose to give up or go on. I would say it hasn't defined me, although all the experiences of our lives define us. I'm all right. There have been moments when things were great sometimes in my life, but I think physically speaking is what people are asking about. Okay is not bad for a guy like me. I can walk...kind of."

Self-deprecation and humor are qualities that enrich Will's life. He gets philosophical about love though. "I'm not sure I know what love is. Other people experience love differently. I know many can turn love on and off which is just a mechanism for controlling the relationship. Turning love on and off is not really love at all. I equate love and giving yourself as one and the same thing. If you don't give yourself, you're not really in love with a person. You can love someone and care for him or her, but it doesn't necessarily mean you're in love with him or her. It's a distinction that's been made many times in the past."

Will has not made a practice of giving much thought to what Will thinks or what Will feels. Does that translate to baggage? He reflects, "I've always been far more interested in what I was doing as opposed to what I was thinking. Is this good or bad for me? I'm more interested in whether it was good or bad for who or what I was dealing with."

Will has a strong work ethic. Does it get in the way of experiencing fully other parts of his life? Is it time to give up work? Will doesn't think so. "Not really. My horrifying fear of losing cognizance does play a part in it. I like to build things. Businesses. One way to keep your cognitive ability is to keep learning, keep doing, and have curiosity and new experiences. It's rewarding. I don't feel that my work ethic kept me from enjoying other parts of my life. I do other things. I probably should have spent more time with my family rather than riding airplanes about the country. But, I don't find fault with people who don't have the same work ethic as I do."

What Will does see as baggage in his life is possibly the ability to not let go of some of the black episodes of his life. He reflects, "I do not forget them, and they come to life more often than they should. I'm not sure that it would be healthy to relieve yourself of all your baggage.

You learn from these things, and you should not forget to listen. Forgetting actual circumstances hasn't worked for me yet. They do pop up from time to time. I relive one in particular at times. "

When asked if black episodes referred to war experiences, he quipped, "War experiences? After decades, I wonder if I'm telling what really happened or what should have happened. I do have a desire to fly under the radar. I don't think my private life is anyone's business but mine. In the parts that I share, I don't need to be the center of attention. My television days were actually a burden to me at times, but I didn't think of myself that way. I was a hard working news reporter."

Will structures his time even while being interviewed. When asked why he does this, he was very straightforward, "Because I have a lot of other things to do. I've done this for years. It's worked for me. I'm self-centered and protective of my time. I'm taking a greater role in the family business and the community business. I can manage my own affairs. I exercise 6-8 hours a week. I know I need to do it. I'm acutely aware of working on the aging thing. If you slow down too much, it's going to overtake you. It's just the way I am. I'm more of a planner than a spontaneous person." Whether that adds up to baggage or a life well lived is not something Will has thought much about.

CHAPTER 4
Non-Conventional Relationships

I woke up in the middle of the night recalling the dire news I had learned that day that Will had been having symptoms indicating possible heart issues. These thoughts swept through my brain seeping into my neck for the exquisite ache to follow. I began to remember…

The Coralie Story

Instinctively, my goal in our relationship had always been to make Will younger. From the time we met, Will had expressed concern about "the difference in our ages." I was aware, he was older, but he didn't look it or act it. A successful businessman, he managed many farms from his computer. I didn't know at the time what that phrase, "the difference in our ages", really meant, but I would come to know. I began to devote myself to a study of aging and how its effects could be altered. I learned that the length could be measured in part by the length of our telomeres, the tiny hair-like protuberances at the end of each strand of mitochondria, the tiny energy factories within our chromosomes. My discovery that one can add to the length of one's life by increasing the length of one's telomeres was all I needed to hear.

A few months after we started dating, Will escorted me to the Fox Theater to see Jersey Boys. Coming home, I decided to tell him that I wasn't ready to kiss him, but I would tell him a story about a kiss. I swallowed my hesitation and jumped in. I told him about telomeres, mitochondria, and how we can lengthen our lives. What is required to jumpstart the process is a visceral reaction in our body. A kiss could start the process if there is chemistry.

The next time we were alone together, I asked Will to close his eyes, and I gently kissed him on the lips. The chemistry was instantaneous. I asked him what he felt upon receiving the kiss. He took my hand and placed it upon his furiously beating heart. It was a soft kiss, and it brought up all these feelings in my stomach. I didn't expect to like it nearly that much. But going forward, I was sure Will's telomeres were growing with each kiss.

Will was overwhelmed, I believed, with the speed with which our relationship was growing. He often lamented, "What am I going to do with you?" It came to pass that references to "the difference in our ages" gained speed.

While he was gone for a week to Lake Tahoe with his family who were shareholders in their farm and urban real estate business, I decided to find out what actually was the difference in our ages. I was 73 at the time, and I learned to my dismay from People Search that Will was 87. I was devastated. My instinct was to cut and run before I got hurt really badly. All week, I dreaded to implement my decision to break off my relationship with Will upon his return. I went into grief mode. By the end of the week, I realized it was way, way too late. I would be hurt whether I decided to stay or go. I was thankful his absence gave me time to work through my dilemma. By the time we reconnected, I had decided to stay and not mention my discovery. In truth, Will thought I knew how old he was.

We continued our relationship, but the difference in our ages seemed to become even more of an issue with Will. As time went by, I grew to hate that phrase. The time came when I visited my brother in Texas where he had recently moved into a senior living center. Will and I had started our book project on living after loss, and I actively pursued meeting people in this environment and paying attention to how they lived their lives. I communicated my concerns to Will by email that I found the atmosphere within the senior living center to be oppressive.

Will has lived in a senior living center for many years although he has his own home within the estate section. Will wrote this while I was in Texas. "I believe we are witnessing God's hand in the lives of Coralie and Will. My intuition tells me you did not go to visit your brother by chance, but it was ordained and meant to be. All to open your eyes to the real world in which Will lives and the wonderful possibility of a mutually supportive, mutually caring, and mutually productive friendship that can be ahead of us. In 47 days, I will be pushing hard on 90 which is not the place for a dynamic woman of 74 with a huge world of possibilities at her fingertips."

It became clear to me that the difference in our ages issue was coming to a head. Will became adamant that he didn't want me to be stuck in his world. He called it his "steely resolve" that our relationship would transition to that of friends and colleagues. Both of us had experienced caretaking at the end of our marriages. Will's caretaking of his wife went on for some 17 years. It changed who he was. He cares enough for me not to let me be stuck in caretaking for him in the present.

According to Will, timing has been an important factor. At one time, he referenced if we had met when we were younger, say 60 and 74, my name would not be the same as it is now. But alas, we were not free at that time and were not destined to meet until we were both much older.

I was not yet ready to give up our romantic relationship. I was still trying to make Will younger. He obviously possessed all the qualities of people who remain vital into their older years. His philosophy of aging includes his determination to never allow other people to do for him what he can still do for himself. I was convinced that the "make Will younger" project was working. He had taken to describing himself as too busy to get old.

But reality is intruding. My best efforts to ignore "the difference in our ages" may have run its course. The recent health concerns Will has described have touched my heart. We are not going to reignite our former relationship. Nor is he willing to make me a widow again. We will see how it goes. In the meantime, what I have learned is to cherish and take care of what you value. Happiness is fragile. Appreciate every moment and do everything you can to protect it. Someday, perhaps I'll understand why the gap difference in our ages made so much difference.

The Beth and Rob Story

The story of Beth and Rob is somewhat different. Although Beth was six and a half years older than Rob, the difference in their ages was not significant, until it was…Rob lost Beth to cancer a few months ago.

Years ago, when they had found each other, both had suffered lossBeth following 14 years of marriage and Rob after nearly four lonely years in the South Pacific serving in the military.

They were both rebuilding the next chapter of their lives in the classrooms of the local university. They were both enrolled in science classes studying geography, geology, and climatology. Beth was not yet divorced with two young children, so their relationship was confined to just talking for the first two years. But Rob remembers there may have been a spark. "We laughed at the same things and had a common interest in the classes we were taking."

Beth got a divorce, and the relationship between Rob and Beth escalated. Rob recalls, "She was a good person. It wasn't purely a physical attraction." Eventually they married. Rob said the fact that she had two young children wasn't necessarily an issue for him. He quips, "I wasn't smart enough to have spent much time thinking about that. When you're smitten, you don't think about practical considerations. The kids didn't bother me. If we had actually thought about things, we may not ever have married.

Rob remembers, "Her mother didn't like me. Her first husband was quite successful and I was a student and ex-sailor." Rob wonders if perhaps Beth's biological clock may have been ticking. Recalling that Beth had been married when she was no more than a child, Rob felt she might have needed to get out of her situation to find one involving more affection. Getting out of her marriage was a huge issue for Beth, he believes. "She was a very careful person. It was a giant step for her."

On the subject of blending families, Rob recognized, "It was not difficult for me. Our son was not like me, but he and I both worked hard at resolving whatever problems arose. On the other hand, our son and Beth were just alike. They both didn't get the same jokes etc., so I provided a foil to their relationship. Our son was the one who requested that I adopt him. We've been pretty good for each other. The adjustment was relatively minor. I like to play with kids, and we shared a love of sports."

When Beth and Rob were first married, Rob worked seven or so years in retail, but Beth wanted a husband who was home nights and weekends. He remembers, "She put the squeeze on me pretty hard to change career paths. " About this time, Rob was advised that his education would qualify him to take the test for a state job. "With my veteran's preference, I was in the top echelon of people applying, and at the time, they were hiring men to balance gender equivalency. We took a trip to the testing area." Staying at a Bed and Breakfast there, Rob struck up a connection with the owner who was friends with the tester. This synchronicity together with Rob's talent for writing allowed him to be chosen for the job. The test had involved supporting and justifying your position on an issue. Rob won't say so, but he has considerable writing ability.

At the time, Rob felt his biggest adjustment was moving from a career where you had to please people to one where you needed to be forceful. He became district supervisor eventually.

Now, all this time, there were not any particular issues of age differences. Everything was copacetic. A sense of humor is one of Rob's personality characteristics. He claims, "Beth and I did darn near everything together, especially early in the marriage. I liked to fish, so we fished together. I liked to camp, so we camped together. Eventually, however, we neither fished nor camped together to any extent. We gravitated to doing more cultural things. We agreed it would be good to do them together. We stumbled into the antiquing business. We stumbled into gardening and cultivating flowers. We looked for things we could do together. We built a life on mutual interests."

Now that he is alone. Rob wonders if he will pursue the same activities. He is becoming more independent and doubts he would be interested in making a lot of concessions. He gets to choose new roles for himself.

Rob thinks it might be significant that his life has changed so much now that he is alone. Before, he recalls, "The only activities we pursued separately were that I played golf and she played bridge. Even so, as a concession to her, I played bridge at times with one group. There was not much we did apart. We did about 90% of our activities together."

They also traveled and researched antiquing. Rob explains, "There was nothing like an auction for Beth. It was the search for treasure that might be out there, an adrenaline high! She searched for a high dollar item and became involved in the bidding process to get it. I remember one time at an auction when she decided she wanted a pineapple twin bed to match the one we had. We spent $150.00 for that item which we didn't have at the time, but it was the pursuit she was connected to. She wanted it, and she came after it. There were very few things she became aggressive about, but searching for treasure at auction was one of those things she was attracted to. One of the last things we did together that held any enjoyment for her was a trip to Ohio to attend an auction."

Propagating flowers, according to Rob was mostly a function of Beth's creativity. Rob concedes, "I don't have any real desire to do that anymore. I have to work at it. She must have been the motivation behind it all, because it isn't there for me anymore without her. I would have guessed that I would have continued that work. It has surprised me that my desire to do that has left me."

Up until the time Beth became ill, Rob revealed that the difference in their ages had not been a factor. He said he would give the difference about a 2% out of 100%. "It wasn't an age difference, it was a health difference. When you lose your health, you lose practically everything. There was hardly any restriction on her activity until near the end of her life."

When Beth's cancer returned, Rob chose to give Beth his full time support. He gave up his gym workouts that were important to him. "There was no choice to be made that I saw. It was not a sacrifice. It was a relatively easy choice." When Beth spoke of her husband's complete commitment to her care, she became tender and would refer to him with a shortened form of his name changing Robert to Rob when she spoke. Rob said, "I didn't know she did that. I never heard her use that diminutive form of my name."

Rob doubts that if Beth had lived to be 85, even then, the age difference would not have been a factor, "It was always health that made the difference. Typically, women live longer lives, so for a man to marry an older woman actually makes sense. The only difference he noted was walking speed. If you're healthy, you walk faster. That's still a health factor though."

Rob regards his marriage as a good one. "It was about as solid as you could get. He thinks it would be hard to get used to someone else again. Now that I'm independent, it might be more difficult to concede ground to a new person. It seems so alien to be around someone else. Other than a friendship type situation, it might be a difficult adjustment. But age difference would not be the deciding factor." And so it goes around and around, but for Rob and Beth, the difference in their ages made little or no difference.

CHAPTER 5
Remarkable Relationships

We never outgrow our need for connection. 90-year-old romance can be viewed as an intriguing cliff off which to plunge into one of their stories. All the people featured in the following stories were in the 90-year-old age group.

The Ira Story

Dr. Ira Kennedy knows about loss. His daughter, Carrie was 20 and one-half. She had been a little slow since infancy. She did graduate high school. She tried college, but dropped out after 3 weeks. She began working at the Lutheran Home as an LPN. She had been reading Life After Life by Raymond Moody. She talked to her parents about the great light at the end of the tunnel. Carrie said, "That's Jesus."

She then went to work. That day she collapsed onto her coworker and died. They did an autopsy. Everything inside her was small. She had a stenosis of the main artery. Ira observed, "We grieved for her, but we realized life would have been rough for her had she lived. She had constant pain in her esophagus."

He remembers, "It snowed 10 days before she died. We had gone to look at cars for her. She picked out a little Honda Civic. She put $25.00 of her own money down on the car. She was very happy."

Ira recalls the spiritual side of acceptance of her death. "At church the next Sunday, a beautiful tenor voice sang, Holy, Holy is What the Angels Sing. That Psalm affected me. I felt changed and inspired by that song. By Friday, I realized it was preparation to lift our hearts from the Lord. We didn't grieve. We just missed her."

There were other losses. Ira and his wife, Emily, were married 55 years. He remembers, "Four days after she had pelvic surgery, my wife said she had to get back to bed. She said she couldn't breathe. An embolism had gone from her leg to her lungs. She wasn't getting enough air, and she died." It was mercifully quick. They had been living at a senior living center. Afterwards, Ira took refuge in a woodworking shop where he could lose himself in woodworking.

Ira reflected on the subject of loneliness. "Ironically, I had experienced extreme loneliness in the 20 years before my wife died. She suffered from mild depression. She took after her mother and refused to get help. She gradually withdrew from conversation. The longest we had was a two-sentence conversation. I missed that. Bang! The doors shut. I would try a sentence 4 or 5 times in my mind thinking how to best get a positive response. I would then try to interest her in some activity.

Her classic response was, "You can if you want to." With great pain, Ira remembers that during the time they still lived in the neighborhood before moving to the senior living center, he experienced loneliness so great that he began to lose his conversational skills. At least at the center he had people to talk to. He recalls, "The highlight of our day was the evening meal. We sat at a table for eight people. The group would feed on each other."

Before she died, Ira's wife had told him, "If I go before you, go ahead and get married." About this time, Betty Jo moved into the apartment Ira now occupies. It was about a year before his wife died. They both noticed she had big surgery scars on her neck. She had lost her husband about two months before. They both thought she must have been a brave person to have been through so much. They were neighbors, and Betty Jo joined them at their table for the evening meal.

Ira recalls, "Betty Jo developed a leaning on me. Another resident and I took her to St. Louis for surgery and doctor appointments. She had cancer in her cheek. There was not a good blood supply so they took a 10 inch strip from her left forearm."

One Sunday morning, Betty Jo asked Ira to come quickly. Her pillow was bloody. Blood vessels had ruptured. He took her to the emergency room. "We neighbored. These incidents brought us together. We developed a connection."

After his wife died, Ira described the sense of having a blank side on his right side where his wife always walked. Her energy provided a tangible loss. But he recalls he would never have called her back.

Ira's relationship with Betty Jo turned toward personal about a year after his wife died. They took a day trip to a museum called the Stars and Stripes. He recalls Betty Jo was curious. "She took an interest in everything. It touched a nerve. She also had a great sense of humor. She and her late husband had posed as clowns at church functions. I began to think we might get married. The next week we went to Big Oak Tree State Park. As we were walking, she wobbled. I asked her if she would like an elbow. It filled that blank spot."

They began to talk of marriage. She asked Ira the question, "Would you want to marry me with all my problems?" I answered her, "In a New York minute! After our Bible study, I got down on one knee and asked her to marry me."

At this point, Ira reflected on almost a sense of relief he had felt after his wife died. There had been little or no communication. Ironically, the only real connection they had was in a physical sense. "We communicated better that way than in words. But even that had to be contrived. I could not approach her directly. In the morning, I would go to the foot of the bed and touch her toe. I would then go up her ankle, leg and shoulder. She began to wiggle, wakened by degrees. She tolerated that. I likened the process to a Black Widow spider asking if I could come in."

Ira is a psychologist. He believes his wife may have been influenced by behavior her Mother modeled. "Her mother was domineering. Emily was soft and responsive at least in the beginning. She was a good conversationalist for the first year of their marriage. "All of a sudden she said, do so and so. I thought this behavior was coming from her mother. "

He says his greatest sadness was in the raising of their children. "I had good ideas as a psychologist for raising children. But Emily felt she should take care of the children. It was better for them to do what their mother demanded. But they all turned out well."

Ira has a daughter who takes him grocery shopping on Mondays. His son is nearby. They spend time with him. Eye problems keep him from driving now.

Ira reflected on his time with Betty Jo. "We were married for five and one half years. All but the last year was good.

She had another surgery. I became the caretaker. She didn't want to go to the Health Center. So, I took care of her physical needs. We knew she was likely to die."

At this point Ira has no plans to seek another relationship. He reflects, "When Emily died, I was starved for conversation. But I really had no desire to marry again. Ours was 98% a good marriage. When I married Betty Jo, I got the other 2%." He is reminded of the Christmas story. When Simian held the baby Jesus in his arms in the second chapter of Luke, he says, "Your servant is ready to die." Ira concludes, "Life has given me everything I need. I don't want anything."

The Lewis Story

Lewis Litwin has been connected to our family for years. He worked side by side with my mother at the Belmont Arboretum where my mother was a volunteer and President of the Tree Board governing body. There is a beautiful arbor constructed in her honor in a prominent location on the 22-acre facility.

Last weekend, I went home. It has been said, "You can't go home again." I did it even though my childhood home across from the old football stadium has long since been torn down to make way for a parking lot. The occasion was my class reunion. Over 250 former graduates came together to share memories even though some of them graduated over 60 years ago.

Lewis is 90, but he was flitting about agilely inviting people to come to the arboretum the next day where he would be conducting tours. He drove people around in his golf cart identifying plants, trees and flowers. A gigantic concrete turtle donated by the old skating rink sits on a concrete foundation in the north end presiding over two miles of walking trails that take visitors through the woodlands.

Lewis is good at relationships. He knows grief and loss. His wife of over 50 years died suddenly one night. She had only complained that she didn't feel well. She awoke in the night again describing her feelings. She passed away before morning. Grief is difficult and lonely, but more so if we are not connected with others.

Fortunately, Lewis was connected and grounded. After a time, he began to search for relationships and travel. Lewis was good at cruises. An amateur magician, in his younger years, he had been able to entertain people in a gig aboard cruise ships. Now, all he lacked was a traveling companion.

About this time, a widow came to our small town in the company of her son, a new dentist to the area. They started keeping company. Gregarious and charismatic, Lewis was able to convince her it would be safe to cruise with him. After all, he enjoyed an impeccable reputation as a church and youth leader. Off they went!

On another occasion, he called my sister from NYC to share what a wonderful time he was having, going to Broadway shows and seeing the sights in the company of yet another widow.

He regularly entertains in his comfortable home where he renewed old relationships by inviting some 27 people to come for ice cream after the reunion banquet and program at the high school. Lewis was just being Lewis when he asked the graduates, most of them over 75, to form a circle. When the last hand connected, lights and sparklers came on as he manipulated a device he was holding to make that happen. How he did this was just one more magician's secret.

He made malts for guests from an old fashioned machine that he had obtained from the confectioner's store where we children would gather 60+ years ago. At the time the store closed, only Lewis would think to purchase and preserve something so dear to our hearts as children. My brother-in-law has Parkinson's. He loves root beer floats so, of course, Lewis made him one from the old ice cream machine that still works perfectly.

On Sunday morning, Lewis presided at church recognizing the graduates that were attending from out of town. Every small town has its share of people who are different. One such person was Neale who always had an innate technology talent. There was some kind of disconnection, however, between his brain and his mouth. He just couldn't articulate what he was thinking very well. But his face lit up when Lewis recognized him as the graduate who served as IT person for the church.

Lewis Litwin is a living example of a life well lived. He lives an empowered life for himself and those whose lives he touches. He has successfully navigated life's challenges with relationships that are deeply satisfying.

The Molly Story

Austin, Texas, psychotherapist, Dave Helms, coined the term "serial relationships" to describe multiple, sequential relationships occurring more often in the lives of older Americans. Since seniors, particularly women, are living longer, healthier lives, increasingly, they are enjoying relationships with three or more people over their lifetimes. Such was the case in the life of Molly.

Molly lived her life with intention: connected to outlets for healthy stimulation of her mind, body, and spirit. I was drawn to her energy. She agreed to meet me in her home where she lived alone, self-sufficient and still vital at near 90. A curious person, she loved to travel, swim and dance. These things were to play a part in her relationships. I was inspired by the courage, resilience, and perseverance she displayed within the challenges she faced.

When Molly's husband, Ken, the father of her three children suffered a massive heart attack and succumbed, it was shocking. Molly was only 43 years old. Her youngest was a junior, soon to be senior in high school. Ken was in the hospital when he died unexpectedly. He had seemed in reasonably good health prior to the attack even though he had health issues following six years in the navy. Molly feels he had PTSD. The minister said he had seen many men with similar issues following WWII but they didn't call it PTSD then.

Molly feels one factor in his eventual death might have been that the many experimental drugs and shock treatments he was given by the VA during treatment were hard on his heart. Molly describes the aftermath: "we dealt with his death the best we could."

When asked at what point she decided to date following the death of her first husband, Molly corrected me saying she never at any point in her life including two more marriages and several relationships decided to date. She was just living her life when relationships happened. She worked for a company called Fabric Mart Draperies.

Her assistant manager set up a double date with Molly and the manager, she and her husband. "It was only four months after my husband died, but I decided it was time to get out."

The manager had many of the qualities Molly valued: "he was nice, a wonderful dresser. His manners were impeccable. The four of us double dated. I agreed to go out occasionally. He had a wonderful sense of humor, was a good dancer. His manager position required him to dress well. I knew him well. He worked with fabrics and knew how to present himself well.

The manager was the only man I went out with prior to meeting the man who would become my second husband. Time went by.

I met the man who would become my second husband through my daughter-in-law. His son and my son had been friends. The son was also John's insurance man. I met his father through some issue about my son, John's, insurance policy. He was helpful to John's widow, but I wasn't looking for anyone. I stayed busy with clubs. The man who would become my second husband was a widower. All my dates and husbands were widowers. He had five children, but they were all grown. There were never problems."

Her second husband-to-be called Molly and invited her to dinner. She said he was charming, a good conversationalist. Molly describes herself as somewhat quiet, easy to get along with. This man was semi-retired, had a summer home on Fox Lake about 40 miles from Milwaukee, but lived in Milwaukee.

"We got married and moved to Fox Lake. My mother and his still lived in Milwaukee. We were only married two years when my second husband died. He had been a smoker, had one room that was an office where he smoked with the door shut and the window open. I think smoking may have contributed to his having a heart attack."

Molly went back to Milwaukee following the death of her second husband. She returned to her job at Fabric Mart Draperies, working her way up to manager.

Molly never actively looked for a partner, but what continued to attract her were good manners, good taste, good dresser, and always dancing played a part. More importantly, she said they were kind, thoughtful, and a lot of fun.

As for her, she describes herself as easy to get along with, dressed nice, and was reasonably attractive. That was an understatement. I saw a picture of Molly on her first wedding day. She was a gorgeous, big-eyed, very attractive woman.

During this time, Molly had a married friend with a home on Ferry Lake. She would visit with her on weekends. Her friend thought she should meet a man in Milwaukee. Molly loved to travel. As a young woman, she had traveled to either coast by train so she was comfortable traveling for several days at a time. Travel and dancing would become a theme in almost all her relationships. She then began dating the man from Milwaukee.

Her friend set Molly up with a blind date with Phillip. When he called her for a dinner date, she asked "Where?" to see if he had good taste. She had certain standards.

In reviewing the important relationships of her life, Molly said her first and third husbands were the loves of her life. The third husband was much like the first. During the second relationship, she was grieving for her son. That gets in the way so much, it's often called the transitional relationship. It can work for a while, but it often doesn't last. Molly was dating another man when she met her third husband.

Molly said, "Phillip and I dated a number of years. We took trips together. My Mother had died. My sister and her husband transferred to Florida. My youngest son, Bill, was living in southern Illinois. He encouraged me to live closer. Phillip passed away about a year after I moved to the mid-west.

I was doing some volunteer work for a professor at a local university. I worked with older people riding in the van. We picked them up, took them to appointments. Another volunteer and I became good friends. She invited me to Christian Singles. There was a man there that liked me. I learned later he took dancing lessons to please me. Traveling, dancing, and swimming are the activities that define me. I was dating him when I met my third husband."

Meanwhile, while working at a children's clothing store, I became the night manager. I was still dating the man I had met at Christian Singles. One of the college girls who worked with me said she would like me to meet her grandfather. She said he likes to dance. She set me up with a blind date with her grandfather. We started dating. We hit it off. I began to be uncomfortable dating two men. I determined I would have to break up with the man from Christian Singles. It was hard to do. I had never had to break up with someone. The Christian Singles guy had made me a cedar chest. I think he was serious.

When I met my third husband, he had had a bad dating experience with a woman who had run up debts and left him with the debt. So his daughter was reluctant to have someone in his life. The daughter trusted Molly eventually. He knew his daughter would want his assets so he made it a point to put everything in both their names. When buying a home, he put Molly's name exclusively on the title. So Molly did have a home following his death after only four years.

They were married in the chapel at a local hospital, as he had a hernia that was starting to strangulate. The doctor said he couldn't leave the hospital. He had to have emergency surgery. But he didn't want to put off marrying Molly. He told the doctor he wouldn't have the surgery until he was married to Molly. He couldn't have champagne. Right after the reception, the surgery nurse threw rice after they brought her husband back to his room.

"We were married only four years. I suffered deep grief. It was no easier than either of the other two losses, but I do not regret it. My faith helped me to move on.

Prior to his death, Molly's third husband developed Alzheimer's. His son had taken his life. After that, it all started. He went through the stages fast. Molly remembers, "I kept him at home as long as I could. Early on, he would be sitting beside me telling me a funny story. In reality, it was something I did, but it was like he was telling a stranger. We were still sleeping together and one night, I was so exhausted I didn't feel him get up. I woke up suddenly hearing a popping noise. He had turned on the electric stove under my copper teakettle that held a little water. The spout popped off. The doctor said I must not keep him at home. I took him to a Jackson nursing home. He was agreeable. He had already developed a difficulty swallowing. He passed away that same evening."

There were subsequent relationships. Molly recalled, "I used to go to Arizona. My son, John's widow lived there with my grandson. I went there during the winter. While there, I met a man who was an architect from Albany, New York . He had a place in Arizona. I dated him after my third husband died. One time, he picked me up in my town in the mid-west and drove me to Arizona. I dated him while in Arizona. The New York architect had never been married. He was interested in me. Later, he told me he had an affair and learned he had a daughter he hadn't known about. He found out he had cancer and died in Arizona

During this time, I was dating another man who liked to dance. He belonged to AARP. He was membership chairman. He wanted me to go dancing in a town about an hour away. There was a Sunday afternoon dance. He mentioned that modern women were sometimes paying their own way. He was hinting. I told him I was old fashioned. I was used to the man paying. After that, he paid for things. I used to have him for dinner at times. I might have married him, but he wasn't the love of my life. I got a call from his daughter while in Arizona for my grandson's 30th birthday that he had died. "

Molly's love of travel led her to considerations of sleeping arrangements if she were to travel with a man who was not her husband. When I asked Molly how she managed sleeping arrangements, she said staterooms usually had single beds or bunk beds. She said demurely she had shared a hotel room with a man at times on travels. It was left unsaid what the arrangements might be. Early on, she said she was somewhat uncomfortable, but she learned to cope with the issue. The first time she traveled with a man, they stayed with friends. She said she ran into couples doing the same thing. She noted financial considerations often dictate not remarrying.

She indicates she gets tired of talking to just women and enjoys the male perspective. She enjoys talking to her son who is almost 65 and a widower in St. Louis. He has dated a psychiatrist, a chiropractor, a nurse, and several teachers most of whom he has met through church. Molly hopes he can find a significant relationship.

Molly just had her 91st birthday. She still swims regularly and remains active. She typifies the senior woman who is living vitally in her older years. Since dancing has always been a part of her life, I found it poignant to learn that Molly recently got back out on the dance floor again to the strains of music from a live orchestra. That zest for experiencing life to the fullest is part of what has kept her going.

That willingness to risk is one of the secrets to successful aging. After burying two husbands, Molly could very well have chosen to protect her heart from ever having to go through that kind of loss again. Instead, Molly has had to bury three husbands. She says none of the losses was any easier than the first. She believes if she had never met them, there would be no weight to carry, but also no memories to sustain her

CHAPTER 6
Let Me Be Me

According to Dr. Henry Cloud and Dr. John Townsend, authors of Boundaries in Dating, "Boundaries define us, show us what we are and are not…The second function of boundaries is that they protect us."

The Jerry and Danielle Story

Boundaries were to play a part in the relationship of Jerry and Danielle. When I stepped into Jerry's new condo, I was startled to note the quality of the artwork and professional décor. His companion, Danielle, is a talented artist and decorator, and the pieces she and Jerry had chosen were impressive. Jerry was quick to note my amazement and observed that his adult children, particularly his daughters, were equally startled when they first saw his new place. Nothing of their mother was left. Which takes us back to 2013…

After a painful illness, Jerry's wife of 57 years and mother of their children passed away. After a successful career in management, Jerry had retired to his work as a clock technician. It was a solitary hobby, however, and Jerry was very lonely. He was in good physical shape and enjoyed bowling, golfing, and later, line dancing.

Danielle had lost her husband a few years before, and was also physically active enjoying many of the same activities. They were destined to meet while bowling in adjacent lanes. Jerry remembers, "I sneaked up behind her at bowling and found out what her name was. It was less than a year after my wife died when I met Danielle. The trait that attracted me, in fact defined her, was her classiness. She's just a beautiful woman, carries herself with so much class, makes decisions with so much class, and speaks with so much class. That's what drew me.

Her inner qualities include honesty, in fact, she's sometimes honest almost to the point of embarrassment. She has a great sense of humor. After you've lived 80 years, there are things you've learned to treasure. When someone comes along that embodies all the womanly qualities you treasure, you're drawn like a moth to flame. For example, I love that she can poke fun at me. We have a back and forth that's fun.

The communication is amazing between us. She comprehends things about me almost before they leave my mind. We can talk for hours. Sometimes, I stop and realize I've never told anyone this before. Nothing is out of bounds."

Jerry reflects about how Danielle has changed his life. "We are about the same age and she brings common experiences to our relationship. Our day to day life is very rich. Never in my life have I liked what I am looking at right here so much. It's opened up all kinds of things in my life that I've never looked at before. Now I can sit and talk to people about designing, something I've never considered before. The level of communication we share is a blessing."

One of the reasons communication is so important to Jerry is his experience during his marriage. "I've spent the last 35 years not communicating. Danielle saved my life. Sharon and I had not communicated nor been physically close. I grew and Sharon didn't. Then menopause came along and finished the job. We were just roommates for the last 25 years of our marriage. I retreated to my clocks and worked all night to relieve it. With Danielle, for the first time in my life, I've got someone I can really talk to on a deep emotional level. I'm totally blessed."

Jerry recalls, "I never got over the loneliness. I would talk to the walls. I couldn't stand to be in a room by myself. The loneliness was really hurting me badly. It was the worst part. I was headed toward ill health and depression."

Jerry and I talked about boundaries. Many times people who have been hurt during childhood or in damaging marriage relationships develop a guardedness or protectiveness surrounding their deepest emotions. It may be hard for them to give or receive love based on those experiences.

Jerry said, "Bingo! That's the way Danielle is. That describes her very well. It's taken me awhile, maybe a year into our relationship to realize the boundaries she protects herself with are not so much about me, as her experience.

It caused some pain at first. It seemed I got way ahead of her in what I wanted from the relationship. This seemed so in terms of caring, and that wasn't really true. It's just that she wasn't showing it as much as I was. I know that now. I didn't know it before.

We're so much alike in what is important to us. Our values are similar. Compromise is what we need to do. My thought process is to take the steps to grow the relationship. My next step would be living together, and that's not happening. Although deep in my feelings my brain wants to move in that direction, I'm holding back. At this point, I'm committed to having fun. Even though I would jump at the chance to make it more than that, I can live with that. That's where we are."

Jerry concedes, "I am okay with the fact that she has many friends and enjoys them. She needs time to herself. That's important to me, not only that she has that, but that I allow her to do that. I know the right direction I need to go in. It makes me sad to think about the things Danielle has gone through in her childhood and in her marriage that cause her to need to protect herself.

Another factor is that Danielle was raised in a family where I love you was not spoken. My family is just the opposite. We're huggers, and we verbalize "I love you." She doesn't know how to do that. There's not a lot of "I love you" in Danielle right now because she was raised without hearing any of that. It's hard for her to show love.

I've got a lot of work to do. There's a big part of me that wants to be with her every single minute, every single day. Part of my brain says to me, "That's not smart, Jerry, and it's not going to happen anyway." I care for her that much. I need to be better at not seeing her for 3 or 4 days and not let her know it's bothering me as much as it does. Even better, I should get over that it bothers me so much not to be with her. I know how dangerous it is for any man or woman to feel owned. I don't ever want to go there. When you're in a relationship, and you feel the way I feel, you need to keep checking on yourself to make sure you're not doing that. I'm constantly working on that, but I slip sometimes. Intellectually, I understand that, but the feelings want to get in there and mix the whole thing up. If you've been very lonely, your feelings say- you won't ever be lonely again if you have someone with you all the time. You even have to guard against sharing those thoughts in a kidding way. It doesn't come across as kidding."

Jerry is optimistic about the future of their relationship. Deep down, he realizes that it's not the other person's job to make you happy. You have to do that for yourself.

We all want to have healthy relationships. But, it's not about changing our lives; it's about changing your mind about your life. When we get our thinking straight, we are more likely to make healthy choices. Establishing boundaries promotes healthy choices.

The Coralie and Will Story

There came a time in my relationship with Will that I learned all about boundaries. The problem was the boundaries he proposed supported HIS thinking. As a result, our relationship was to change from romantic to friends and colleagues. It seemed I didn't get a choice in the matter. Perhaps the difference in our ages played a part. Will was older and wiser, at least he believed himself to be so. There's no question he had stronger resolve, more altruism. A man of strong character, with his experiences as a caretaker, he didn't want me to get stuck in his world, that of a senior living complex. He had experienced how that burden could affect you. He never regretted or second-guessed the years he spent caring for his Mother, his aunts, and his late wife. There was never an ounce of self-pity. His strength was his faith in God.

I, on the other hand, wanted what I wanted. His intellect, accomplishments, and strong character set a very high bar. I had yet to experience, for myself, the freedom that boundaries offer. I clung to my belief that you didn't just give up on someone because the situation was not ideal. Yes, he was 14 years older than me. Yes, I had not yet experienced any other relationship since my late husband passed away. To me, great relationships are great because both people care enough about each other to find a way to make it work. I do think it is good for a relationship for thoughts to be expressed. It shows confidence in the other person and doesn't allow for a buildup of suppressed emotion. Patience was the best remedy for every trouble.

So I determined to be patient and to give this friendship thing a chance. What actually occurred is that for a long time, I carried my sadness around like a brick, grieving the loss of our physical intimacy. I tried to accept the boundaries Will established. Time did not kill the attraction we felt for each other. What resulted was a lot of backed up emotion on both our parts.

Fortunately, I began to wonder how much more time I wanted to spend reacting to circumstances rather than creating new opportunities for myself. We both soldiered on with the practical tool of boundaries present most of the time. You cannot go through life without authenticity or at least, it's not healthy to do so. You have to pay attention to your own wishes, feelings and desires. We tried to be honest and purposeful. Will offered unrelenting support and encouragement to my book project. I responded to that like a flower. Soon I was traveling, getting to interview people and forming new relationships. My world was enlarging. What I thought possible for my life gradually increased.

The time came when I made an intellectual decision, supported by Will, to enlarge the way I looked at personal relationships. A very wise woman shared her experience with me that traveling gave you the space to change. But you have to be willing to take the first step.

I overcame my misgivings and made a decision to travel to Aruba for almost a month with four other high school classmates. I recognized, almost immediately, that Jake, one of the classmates, was pursuing me and wanted more than a friendship relationship. That's when I discovered, for myself, the value of setting and maintaining healthy boundaries.

Jake began telling me he loved me almost immediately upon our arrival on Aruba. That's when I realized boundaries were going to be sorely needed. He thought he knew me because of the person he'd known more than 50 years ago. He was also vulnerable. Lee, the love of his life, had passed away several years ago, and Jake was deeply lonely. God created us with a drive to connect, but dating is not the kind of relationship that cures loneliness. It takes time. Relationships don't work well when you take shortcuts.

Feeling the need to be authentic, I communicated to Jake that if he continued to press me, I would push back. We needed to have enough talks for me to feel safe opening up to him. He agreed to respect my boundaries, but he didn't stop telling me he loved me every day. He also told me I was beautiful. I made a decision to stop wearing make-up and using hair products. Instinctively, I was trying to slow things down any way I could. I felt taking your time was a necessary part of developing a relationship. We needed time together and time apart to think things through.

It was nice to have someone quietly anticipating what I might need or want. Whether it was a cup of coffee in the morning, a bottle of water always at the ready as our day progressed, or a glass of wine in the evening, these things kept magically appearing. Deliberately slowing down the pace became my modus operandi.

It came to me that Jake might be confusing who I am now with who I was early on. When I was 10-12 years old, I was pretty much out of reach as far as boys were concerned. I was taller than them, smarter, and I could run faster. I think, unconsciously, Jake may have confused me with who I was then. This image of me needs to be updated, grounded in present reality.

Boundaries, in the present, assist me in taking responsibility for my life and relationships. They are part of the essential processes that make people grow. I look forward to a journey whose experiential implications lead me deeper and deeper into the discovery of what's out there. If I find what I'm looking for along the way, that's just an added bonus; it's the journey that is important.

CHAPTER 7
Reaching Out:
The World of Online Dating

Although online dating appears to be the go to way for people to connect, I believe it is a poor way particularly for seniors to find love. According to Key Sun Ph. D with the Justice and Responsibility League, "Online dating lacks the basic ingredients for developing real love. The most evident problem involves its use of several categories for the dater to predict…the success of their further interactions with one another. This type of artificial contact contradicts the process of meaningful interpersonal interactions, which generate love and attraction."

Kaley's story illustrates the difference between a real love relationship and the results from online dating.

The Kaley Story

When she first met Paul, the love of her life and eventually her husband for 27 years before he passed away, she wasn't ready to get married. "I went home and told the family Paul would be the one. He went home and told his family the same thing. We each didn't know the other had said anything. He worked on the river, so when he disappeared for 30 days, I didn't know what to think. I checked out the bars in his hometown, while he was checking out the bars in mine."

Returning home from the river, he found Kaley in a bar and said, "I've been looking for you." They dated the equivalent of six months accounting for his time on the river. Kaley confesses, "He's the only man I've ever lived with. In your younger years, you will do things you wouldn't normally do. We hid it. Values were, back then, that you don't do that sort of thing." This seems to contrast with societal values now.

According to Kaley, "He was the love of my life. We got married. We had some trouble early on, as most couples do. And we were able to get over that rocky patch by working as a team. Our two children were born nine years apart. I had trouble maintaining a pregnancy. There were seven pregnancies and two live births."

Kaley was thankful for one full pregnancy. She didn't want to ruin her health trying continuously. Eventually though, she became pregnant again. She could have worn one of those sweatshirts that said, "40 and pregnant."

She remarks about the present, "He's a total blessing and total surprise. If not for Clint, the second son, I probably wouldn't have gotten out of bed when Paul passed. He gave me purpose for living. He was 14 when his Dad passed away. You wonder why? Why did that happen when a boy needs his Dad the most-when he was a teenager?, We made it through."

Their lives had changed in 2000. Paul was diagnosed with Hepatitis C. He didn't know he had it. Paul's brother had a massive coronary and dropped dead. Kaley explains what followed which changed their lives. "We decided to have him checked out. His heart was fine, but we learned he had Hepatitis C. When he was 14 years old, he cut off his toe with a lawnmower. He had to have two units of blood. That was before they were screening for Hepatitis C. I remember selling my blood in college. Who knew what kind of blood people were getting at that time?"

Paul went through the treatment, but he didn't respond. He then went to a teaching hospital in St. Louis and joined a research project to figure out what was going on in order to help people with Hepatitis C. Only 4% of people have that condition morph into primary liver cancer. Yet, that's what happened to Paul. They do a biopsy every year. The second year, they found liver cancer. They couldn't do a liver transplant because they already knew the cancer had spread through his body. It was on a vein. They couldn't resect any of his liver because he wouldn't have enough left to live on.

This is where the story could have turned tragic. He was given two years to live. He lived 22 months. Kaley recalls, "We lived with intention. We let the small stuff go-we were going to focus on how good life is. Paul was amazing. His co-workers would ask how he could walk around smiling and be pleasant when he knew he was dying. He would tell them that it was because he knew the Lord and knew he was going to be all right. We lived our life with one foot in faith, the other, in reality. If God wanted to do a miracle, that was okay, if not…. He was on hospice for 21 days. When he went on hospice, we told the kids we weren't going to get the miracle we'd hoped for. They still didn't realize how dire it was until they saw how sick their Dad was. He died at home."

Kaley observed, "Faith has had a major part in my marriage. I was churched before, but not a born again believer. We were evenly yoked in not being followers of Christ, and then we both became followers together. That's remarkable.

Prior to his passing, Kaley saw the handprint of God on so many things. Their older son had been working in Arkansas. Kaley remembers, "He came home on a Thursday for the first time in months. Paul grilled hamburgers. It was our last supper. It was a nice evening. At 5:00 the next morning, Paul suffered a stroke, and by 10:30am, he was gone. That's who Paul was. He would not have wanted to linger, have people looking at him. So, that was fateful. That last night he was outside trying to hang up a flag. I asked him to wait until tomorrow, but, of course, there was no tomorrow.

That was six and a half years ago. Kaley reflects, "It took me that long before deciding to move on. I was not ready for quite a while because my thinking was, how do you improve on that? People have said the highest compliment to your deceased spouse is to date again and get married. I said I didn't think so. I'm very independent. I don't need a man to validate me, to complete me, to get me through life. I was not ready to replace Paul. I felt that way for years. Additionally, my boys would not have been ready for that, but when I finally did decide to date, they thought it was about time."

Kaley feels time heals a lot of wounds. Looking back, she notes, "When my husband died, my older son left, and we really didn't know where he had gone. My younger son reflected that he had not just lost his Dad, but his older brother as well. His brother had just checked out, traveled around the country. He was everywhere. I didn't think I could be any more heartbroken."

Kaley feels she is a strong person. She remembers she got on her knees several times praying that God would get hold of her oldest son. "However you can do it." So he got arrested. She was taken aback after praying that. But she realized that worked. Then, her youngest was diagnosed with a chronic illness. There was just wave after wave in our lives. It took time to recover."

Kaley, finally, was ready to move on with her life. She explained, " I chose online dating because if the only place you go is work and church, there's not much opportunity. There were a couple of much older men in the church, but I was not interested in that, and I don't know whether they would be interested in me. At any rate, no one came forth to show an interest, so after much nagging from my friends and my sister, I decided to try the online thing."

Kaley explains what followed, "I met three people that I at least wanted to meet for coffee or something. I talked for a while with the first person I met. I never gave out my phone number to the first two people. The way it works is you just get a message from the website. It's completely up to you whether you even want to give out your email. The first guy, I wanted to run away from five minutes after I got there, but I stuck it out for a time. I was very nervous and prayed before going to meet him that God would make it clear to me what I needed to know about this man.

I hinted I wasn't interested, but he didn't get the hint. He asked, how about this? And how about that? I told him, if you want me to coach you on other relationships, I could do that, but I'm not interested. He started saying weird things. Within the first few minutes, he started talking about his church. It sounded like a very unusual church, and he does not have the beliefs I had. He kept saying he didn't want to talk about this, but I encouraged him by saying I was glad he was addressing this subject because I needed to know about this stuff. That was the end of that."

The second online meeting didn't go much better. Kaley explains, "I met another guy. He lived 120 miles away so we met at a restaurant that was halfway in between our homes. It struck me that he described being retired but did nothing. I asked him what he did with his time.

He described watching TV, fiddling around in the yard. I thought, that's not living, that's just wasting your time. I didn't have anything in common with him." That ended foray number two into online dating for Kaley.

By way of contrast, the guy Kaley met next and dated for two months was a very nice man, pretty honest, and a good conversationalist. Kaley recalls, "We could talk for hours about anything at all. He was very smart, really intelligent and had a good sense of humor. He was from Illinois I asked him if he was from Illinois, did that mean he was in the Mafia?"

He shot right back at me, "So, we're doing it this way?" Starting off this way was fun for Kaley, exhilarating even. Kaley remembers, "He was a gentleman, opened doors for me, was really polite. This was the first time I really had any attention from a man in years. It was the first time in 34 years that she had gone out with someone other than her late husband. It was heady. I got carried away. We would talk each night on the phone for an hour. We never ran out of things to say. He was the only person I gave my cellphone number to.

From the profiles, I had learned we lived fairly close and were approximately the same age. He was a year younger. He loved his kids. What I discovered as we drove around was that he cast himself as a victim. He would point out where he used to live until his ex wife took everything. He would tell me he built that house but lost it. He lived in the past lamenting what he used to have. Or he lived in the future telling me he was going to do this or going to do that. I really didn't want to see the truth at first because I was having fun. But then, the turning point was that my conscience would not let me rest.

Since then, I have realized it probably would not have gone very far. I didn't think he was financially stable. Also, he was a little over connected to his children. He talked to all five of his kids every day. He and his kids were a lot more open with each other than I was used to. His oldest daughter called him and said she thought she was going to have an affair because her husband wasn't satisfying her. Can you imagine your kid calling you and saying something like that? I thought, wait a minute, are there any boundaries here?"

Kaley began to think there was something squirrelly about his relationship with his kids. "I asked him what he told his daughter. He said he told her she needed to talk to her husband. That was a good answer, but it gave me pause."

Kaley began to reflect on the relationship and what she had learned. "I need to follow up my words with behavior. When our relationship first began to be intimate physically, I told him I didn't do this without a commitment. "

He said, "By commitment, do you mean marriage?" "I told him yes, but then backed away from the line I had drawn. I started out strong. I need to stay firm in what I want, what I need. I called him on the phone. I told him that I didn't feel I owed him a trip to his house to say I couldn't do this anymore. I thanked him for letting me know I was still attractive to a man, that a man could be interested in me. I wished him all the best."   I think we did have an exclusive relationship during those two months, but I'm not sure it would have lasted. There were other things. It troubled me that in his profile, he had represented himself as owning his own business, but that had actually changed two years before. He didn't update his status. He was living in the past."

He asked, "Can't we be friends?" I replied, "No, I have to protect myself. A month later, he dropped by my house. I asked him what's up? He told me he just wanted to see how I was doing. I think he just wanted to see if we could be friends. I told him that would not be good for me. I needed a clean break. "

Kaley analyzed whether she felt online profiles were usually accurate. She noted that was hard to answer. "No one can include everything. Of course, you're going to be selective about what you share. My profile said I'm looking for someone who is a follower of Christ and walks out his or her faith. I put it out there on Christian Mingle. I did it for a month. There are scammers out there. I'm pretty perceptive so I can usually spot an exaggeration." Kaley described one response, "I can tell I would care for you from the bottom of my heart." During her career, she worked with juvenile offenders. She said, "I was always looking for, what's the real story? Men go on Christian Mingle looking for women like me, but many are not godly men. They want women of character, but they're not necessarily men of good character. My suspicious mind asked who knows if they have nothing better to do? Maybe they're just playing around. That's hard. Are they really interested in meeting someone, or do they just want to say they have six women talking to them!"

Kaley feels reading many profiles has made her more discerning. She remembers, "At one point, I was talking to two men at the same time. I realized I couldn't do that. I couldn't keep it straight what I've said to each. I needed to focus on one person at a time." She acknowledged that online dating is very confidential. Everything is done through the website. The person decides if they want to take it to a different level. She described the way it works.

"On Christian Mingle, I would receive a message saying so and so sent you a smile. By the time I went to answer it, they had already taken his profile down. They have people working the websites, looking for scammers. It's a protective function they try to put in there. It's really hard, though, because if people want to be devious, they're going to figure out a way to do it. But they try. The website will send you a message if suddenly a profile disappears. They tell you, if you're unable to read a message, it's because the sender's profile has been removed. This happened several times. I had taken a screen shot and sent it to my sister about a suspicious message. By the time I went back in, his profile had been taken down."

Kaley was also able to tell if a message was coming from a person whose first language was not English. "You can spot it with poor grammar or expressions that are out of date. They will try clichés, trying to be westernized, but they don't ring true. They give themselves away with incorrect references. Maybe they are trying to find someone to marry who is a citizen so they can stay here, who knows?"

Kaley does feel God has plans for her life. She's just not sure those plans include another relationship. She notes, "There are women who were in loveless marriages. If I can't have a second chance, I want them to have their first. I've had a good run at a relationship. Sometimes, I think, give that opportunity to someone else; then there's other times when I think, no bring it on! I hold things loosely. I do believe God gives you the desires of your heart eventually. For example, I always wanted more than one child. Problems occurred. As soon as I let go of that, I was pregnant with no problems.

I see myself as an unclaimed treasure right now. I figure no matter where I go or who I meet, I will have a lot to offer. A personal relationship? I'm happy with who I am.

Times have changed. When the Internet was still in its infancy, less than 1% of Americans met their partners though dating sites. By 2009, 22% of heterosexual couples reported meeting online, according to one survey. Kaley's story points out some of the pitfalls of online dating.

The Dale Story

Dale first introduced me to the world of online dating from a male point of view. The male perspective on online dating shows a gender difference. Whereas, women weigh income more than physical characteristics, men are often seeking physical attractiveness. They may mislead women in their profiles as to their income and status. Women were often seeking only a companion. Men on the other hand, may be looking for a physical relationship. Both men and women may be hiding baggage in their profiles. Unresolved issues and emotional pain may accompany them. This could be hard to spot in a profile. Dale claims that especially in large metropolitan areas, this type of connection is prevalent. The world of social media is fascinating as evidenced in Dale's story.

Family rules are predicated on one set of rules according to Dale. Family is over there and romantic is over here. The set of expectations is different. Dale recalls, "My first influence was my mother. I essentially had no father from the time I was seven months. My mother pretty well shut down. These were unfortunate and devastating circumstances for me. All of my upbringing, she did not have it in her to be emotionally available. I never had the security of emotional connection. I've been chasing that ever since. In the larger world, I'm on the fringe of community, not in the center. I've been trying to fill that need ever since. "

Dale married very young when his girlfriend became pregnant. "I entered that marriage knowing it was doomed, but felt I was doing the right thing. That marriage lasted less than one year. At that point, I was going to college. I met my second wife in college. We dated five years before marriage. I made a connection with her family. Unfortunately, the family was what I really wanted, not her. That marriage lasted 20 years. We had two children."

"I realized she was somewhat like my mother in that she was not emotionally available to me, just the children. I chose to end our marriage. I have been chasing emotional connection all my life."

Dale experienced when you don't understand yourself as an adult, the divorce rate is high. "My wife was a restrained person," Dale observed, "and I appreciated that. She was calm, together. It was 17-18 years before voices were raised. Our differences just got put under the rug. Discussing issues was always difficult. Avoidance has always been my modus operandi. The marriage ended in 2001 when I walked away. I sat the children down on their grandmother's porch to tell them I was leaving."

Breaking up a marriage has consequences. The children are affected, and there are great feelings of loss.

Dale acknowledges there wasn't a sincere effort to repair his marriage at the end. This was the beginning of perhaps a dozen on-line relationships he was to have after 2001. He was not without a relationship after that. He believes after 25, on-line is the only kind of relationship there is. Beyond 25 with full time jobs, that's how people hook up has been his experience. He confesses, "I met someone on-line while I was still married to my second wife. Without seeing a single photo of her, I left my family to go be with her. That's how desperate I was for a relationship."

Dale thinks that's a very effective way to meet someone. He says there is a lot of subterfuge. He observes, "Men will typically lie about their height, women about their age. Women will say they're 55 if they're 60. Men will typically put down an age range. If a man is 60, he will list his acceptable range as 35-62. Usually men are interested in women 15-25 years younger than them." He uses as an illustration a man of 70 he personally knew who met and married a woman 30 years younger. His own observations are, "Younger women don't speak my language. Everything is culturally different. I would find it easier to date interracially than to date a much younger woman."

Dale did find a significant relationship that was not on-line during this time period.
"I have had three serious relationships since my marriages. I have come to believe in pheromones. I won't have a relationship if the pheromones are not compatible. It can never develop into a romantic relationship without them. Do the research. Pheromones are much more significant than I originally thought. I do have a willingness to explore a relationship to see if there are enough commonalities. Pay attention to the things that bug you about a person. Young people have less chance of staying together. They haven't developed a tolerance. If a woman has been abused, I have learned she will never be available. She will always be scarred. A woman who has been abused will always have the

need to be in control. I met such a woman. She put on her dating profile, 'Let our scars fall in love.'"

Dale says he is more often interested in women from another culture. 6-9 of the women he's dated were foreign. He's desperately seeking emotional connection. Dale is adamant, "If I don't get back the same degree I'm giving, I think there's something wrong with me."

"I will avoid things. I don't want to hurt someone's feelings. It became a case of my mind using my mouth without giving it permission. Why am I attracted to those that have been so hurt? They're loving, kind, but scarred. They don't trust men. I always think: I'll show them. They'll embrace me. Going forward, I will trust my instincts. I will recognize what I'm really seeking. I'll find, not someone who wants to, but someone who can. Everyone needs the same things I do." Dale brings a lot of emotional baggage to relationship.

In the end, Dr. Grace Harlow Klein, Ph.D. psychotherapist at the Center for Human Encouragement, Rochester, New York may be right. She says, "I believe in the potential for growth, that our lives can be better, that change is possible, that relationships can be deeply satisfying. Connecting with oneself and others are our most deeply felt needs."

Whether daters can find what they want in a mate online varies with the individual. Information found online isn't necessarily useful in identifying a partner.

The Derek Story

The three people I interviewed who had experienced online dating had used christianmingle.com. Ironically, none of the three found any Christians. Derek changed his approach. "I've made unsuitable choices. I looked at the surface qualities but didn't look underneath. And I did it 3 times. With the ones that came later, I've tried harder. Now I'm looking at qualities like a strong faith. In the past, I've looked at the wrong things. We project what we desire. We accept what we see and what we want."

Derek admits, "Yeah I'm vulnerable to rescuing. I rescued all three of them. I'm still doing that. I've been rescuing people all along. So I've looked back on a life of rescuing. I didn't think I was rescuing her when I married her. I've learned I'm making different choices. Like becoming a Christian. I became Mr. Conservative Christian. If you have faith, you have faith. But faith is a marginal thing. You have to see if it's real. People go to church because they're not spiritual-they go to learn. People need to be trained up. To be reborn is to find joy and laughter. If you're not joyful in attitude, how can you be joyful to other people?"

Derek observes, "But I'm still rescuing people. I've done it all my life. I think it's part of what I'm supposed to be doing. I don't try to be judgmental. I've been on Christianmingle.com twice. When it came to the part where it asks if there's something you'd like to add, I explained my situation. I got zero returns. I guess all the Christians were taken, out there. I've relaxed my attitude. It's something I've given God control of. We'll see."

CHAPTER 8
Resilience

It is important to share our stories about resilience so that people can be inspired to move through their loss with hope. These innermost experiences will direct the lives of people to what can come after loss. It can show us how to master life's greatest challenges. We can become stronger. We can learn to face whatever comes to us calmly and courageously. We sometimes do this by observing the example of another as in the following story, which tells about moving from great loss to the sunshine of a second life.

The Brenda Story

Brenda married the father of her children when they were in college. They were married for 13 years. Brenda recalls. "My husband was sick. He had testicular cancer. We went to MD Anderson for cancer treatment. It was a great strain on our marriage. My parents thought that's why I stayed with him, but in truth, I believed marriage was forever, no matter what. I just woke up one morning and decided that since he was never there, I would have to raise my children alone on my own, anyway.

Everything he did was for other people. I was on the bottom of his list. One day when he was playing golf I began to think differently. He played golf a lot because he could drink and play. When he returned I asked him to pick between the bottle and me. He picked the bottle. We got a divorce."

It was 10 months before Brenda met and married Leonard. Brenda remembers, "I wasn't looking for anybody. Tennis brought us together. I didn't want to date, but I was comfortable playing tennis, and that arrangement worked.

He was very, very nice to me, which my former husband wasn't. I really liked that. When Brenda and Leonard were married, her children were 4 and 6.

He was 16 years older than me. He had been married 24 years and had three grown sons. Aligning our new family produced some issues. Being a lot older than me, he had very different ideas on how to discipline. We had no arguments except about my kids. Fortunately, he left the disciplining to me. One of my sons was difficult, one easy. The older one needed no discipline. My younger son had issues all during his growing up years." This was to be a pattern. Brenda told her husband, "Leonard, you can't discipline him. You don't love him enough to discipline him."

Brenda's younger son irritated Leonard. Brenda feels that dealing with her younger son was well worth the extra care because he's wonderful now. Brenda remembers, "Leonard and I were happy together until he got sick. He was a good husband, a good provider. We loved each other very much. He was somewhat of a loner, very involved in his work. The difference in our ages was not an issue early on, but as he aged, I began to realize that part of the reason we disagreed on things was because we were looking at it from different generations. After he got older and sick, he got very negative. That was a problem. An example arose over work we were doing in our home. I wanted wood floors. He did not. I was looking at it from my generation and he from his. Our perspectives were often different due to cultural influences. My family was a little more affluent than his. This caused a different perspective of looking at things."

As time went on, Leonard began to show evidence of problems. Brenda describes that Leonard had always been quietly aggressive, protective of his family and those he loved. He was mild mannered unless crossed. So later, the things that came to be arose from those tendencies that were always there in some form. Brenda recalled, "A few weird things occurred, but we would laugh them off. An example arose one day when Leonard went to the grocery and got behind a lady in the express check out lane. A lady in front of him had tons of coupons, and then she spilled them on the floor. He was livid from the beginning. He got into a shoving match with her husband. I wasn't there and only heard it described from his perspective. I never thought too much of these incidents until he retired. I learned from co-workers after the fact that he was having trouble at work."

Brenda acknowledged that Leonard had an aggressive personality even though he was very quiet. His illness enlarged and emphasized traits that were there. She was desperate to find people to help. Once Leonard was in a nursing home with Alzheimer's, she saw evidences of aggression with others diagnosed with the disease. Brenda recalls, "I observed a woman who went after a man with her cane even though she was medicated. I believe they're happier if they're behaving so some medication is warranted in my experience."

Leonard's diagnosis was Alzheimer's with psychotic tendencies. She recalls, "He threatened the caretaker. He tried to throw a chair through a window. His filter was gone as to what was appropriate. When he entered the nursing home after two years of me caring for him in our home, he confronted the administrator and demanded to know who was going to take care of his sexual needs. He would call and threaten me telling me he knew where I was, and demanding that I come and get him. I finally

97

became afraid of being at home with him as things escalated."

Prior to giving up her efforts to care for Leonard in their home, Brenda recalls he went downhill very fast. She talked to psychologists, his family doctor, and his children. She didn't make a fast decision. Her family doctor felt she might have been able to keep him at home longer if she hadn't already been dealing with her parents for so long.

The way Brenda describes it, "my well had run dry. I had a lot of patience during the ten-year period I dealt with my parents, but the pressure built up in me, the vessel until it finally spilled over into despair. I couldn't deal with Leonard's issues. It was cumulative. My father had macular degeneration. He couldn't see well enough to manage the bills. At the same time, my mother was starting to do things that made us think we were dealing with some kind of dementia or Alzheimer's. My relationship with my mother had always been somewhat difficult. I don't think she liked me very well. Eventually, my father reached a point where he was somewhat afraid of her because she would get so mad at him. They were very social. They had dinner parties, and she loved to entertain. But when she tried to entertain, she would end up frustrated and furious with him. I don't know whether she ever hit him, but I suspect she did. I told him to tell me if she became violent, but he was embarrassed."

She finally was formally diagnosed with Alzheimer's. Brenda read in the 36 Hour Day that if an Alzheimer's person is having difficulty driving, and you let them continue, if they have an accident, they could be wiped out financially. About this time, her Dad told her he was afraid to ride with her, so she took her to have a driver's test in a small area where she could be comfortable driving. "She failed the test. She became very angry with me over losing her driver's license. It was like herding cats. I could never get ahead of the curve. It was always damage control. She would call me to convey she had lost her credit card. I would find it, but she would lose it again. She would sneak around and get another credit card. The issues were constant."

One of the most bizarre stories Brenda related involved her parents' love of travel. There was an agency within walking distance of their home. They would arrange for a trip, pay for it, and be traveling before Brenda could stop it. She recalls, "One time they actually traveled to Egypt. I don't know how they did it. Someone, there, must have helped them. When they came home, I would pick them up at the airport. My father, who had heart issues, would look like he was ready to have an attack. They had lost their car. He related a story about leaving their bag in NYC. Every single day, there was something. So I moved them to a facility, which was independent care. It should have been assisted living, but my Mother wouldn't allow that. A lot of stuff happened. My Mother would call and say my Father had moved out. He was in the next room."

About this time, to complicate things, her son and his live-in girlfriend were living with them. Brenda was taking care of their daughter. All those times she was going to meet her Mother's needs, she was driving across town with a little child. It was hard for her to do both. 'They didn't realize how hard it was for me. The worst part of it is it went on and on until I was depleted.'

There were factors that allowed Brenda to survive almost more than a human can bear. She recalls, "I do suffer from anxiety, and I am taking Paxil already. Early on, I was taking the maximum amount, and I was glad I had it. The administrator of the assisted living facility my parents eventually went into stopped me and said not to take this wrong, but she thought I probably needed professional help to deal with it all. The psychologist did help me. When someone tells me I need help, I believe him or her. The administrator observed the pinched look always present on my face. I did go into support groups at Memory Care. A psychologist helped me deal with guilt. I did have doubts as to whether I had done the right thing, and the ensuing guilt was debilitating. I finally had a meeting with the whole hospice team at the end of Leo's life. Even though they told me I had done the right thing and needed to get on with my life, I felt some guilt."

As often happens, Leonard's children were just glad Brenda was dealing with it and not them. Brenda laments, "I had friends, but I felt I used them up. I was totally consumed with what I was dealing with. The last year of my Father's life, he fell all the time. We probably went to the emergency room 30 times. I didn't sleep. I'm just now getting to the point where I sleep again. Dealing with their insurance, meds, later on hospice, that was my life. I was consumed by it. I felt like the Angel of Death. My Father had fallen after choking on a pill earlier in the day. I went to the hospital. They said they couldn't keep him restrained because it was against the law. He got up, hit his head on the hardwood floor, and had a brain bleed. He developed intestinal C Diff. they put him on hospice, gave him what he needed to be comfortable, and let him die. I am an only child. It was my responsibility. I later philosophized on my situation reflecting, the good news is that you are an only child. The bad news is that you are an only child."

What added to Brenda's psychic pain was that her mother's story was equally awful, too. "The end result was that I had to let her die. Later, Leonard developed COPD. He wouldn't take the medicine. He worsened. I had to decide to let him die. That is why I felt like the Angel of Death."

What happened after Leonard's death was too much change, too soon. Brenda remembers, "I closed on my house at 9:00am. At 1:00, Leonard died. That was a Friday. On Saturday, we planned the funeral. On Sunday, we started moving me. On Monday, the movers came. On Tuesday was the viewing. On Wednesday was the funeral. This rapid change and trauma was a time period I don't honestly know how I got through."

Brenda had a moment with Leonard after his death. I said to him, "I hope I did right by you, Leonard." She reflects, "I was relieved to have all of them in Heaven. That's all I had done for so many years. It was a real relief. I did realize I had done the best I could. I had no real regrets nor would I have chosen to do anything differently. It's taken me some years to realize it."

Brenda takes stock of her life in the present. "I made it! I survived! I don't really want a strong male connection now. If I had a man in my life and a favorite chair I was enjoying sitting in, I would offer him my chair. I would give in to make him happy. My happiness would depend on his happiness. That's how I lived my life. I don't want to do that anymore, but I know that I would. That's how I'm made. It's too much work. I don't want to have to ask anyone's permission for anything. With both my husbands, my happiness depended on whether they were happy with me. I don't want to live like that anymore. I can see myself having a friend, but I would never, ever get married again.

It's too much work, constant worrying about someone else. I don't want to have to worry about someone else."

There are many joys in Brenda's life in the present. "I play tennis several times a week. We counsel each other. We connect. We talk, laugh, and try to be helpful to the ones who are going through similar things. I play bridge. We talk. I still see old friends from my career days. I go to church. I am involved with my nine-year-old granddaughter. I enjoy being alone. I would like more alone time than I have. I know I need to be with other people, but I am at peace with my life.

Brenda's resilience may only be superseded by this amazing story of courage.

The Dolores Story

While I was dealing with a very advanced illness, my husband, Maury, reported not feeling very well. I needed to make a trip for treatment. Maury said, "Let's just get you on a plane and I will deal with not feeling well." Maury thought he was dealing with some kind of unusual flu. About that time, I asked this friend who was also a priest to check on Maury.

Then, like the Titanic, about 10 crazy things went wrong. Maury had been emailing his brother that he wasn't well, but his brother was busy and wouldn't talk to him. Maury was reaching out to others because I was so unwell. When he went out with friends, they reported to me that his head dropped, and he was gone. Whether he had a heart attack or a massive stroke, I don't know. They asked if I thought an autopsy was in order. They were working on him. The ambulance was there promptly. He had no pain; he was just gone.

I didn't want to see him cut to shreds. Was it the right decision not to have an autopsy? I don't know. I wanted it to be handled as a sacred thing. According to our faith, a Rabbi was called for Mikvah, a spiritual bath to prepare for burial. His body was not left alone for a second."

Dolores was in shock. When asked if she had any awareness, things were so dire with Maury, she said she thought she did, "I wouldn't have called my friend, the priest to check on him otherwise. I had a dream that gave me a sense of calling about it. I don't hold a grudge for anyone about the way it happened. He was dead in a millisecond. You can't fix it."

During the year previous to his death, Dolores thinks Maury might have had some awareness he was experiencing a terrible diagnosis. Maury said at some point, "I could have a heart attack and die tomorrow." Dolores noted, "On his computer, he meticulously left the numbers of every account we had together. I don't know how to read it whether he had a premonition." This all happened four and a half years ago.

Dolores thinks these things do happen. She reports having a dream four days before her diagnosis, "Death is coming for me." She went through major treatments. She refers to all that was happening to her at the time of her husband's death as tangled bunches of balls of yarn: the grieving, the physical pain, and the treatments.

She described the aftermath of the death of her husband: "We sat Shiva for seven days. You can't start sitting Shiva

until the body is buried. You bury within 24 hours.
Nothing is done to the body. It is put in a pine box. Then
the mourning begins. The mourners are the wife, the
children, the brothers, and the parents. You're treated as if
ill. Nothing is expected of you. Mirrors are kept covered.
Food is brought to you. The door is open. People come
and go for seven days. At the end of the process, your
friends come. They take you back into life. It is all very
specific. Friends took me for a walk in the neighborhood.
You are then expected to participate in life. I went to a
bereavement group. Everything is intentional for 30 days.
For a year, there are no parties. I believe it protects the
mourner. It was a very intelligent grieving process. I gave
myself over to it."

Dolores learned a lot about herself during the aftermath.
She came to insights about life and about the relationship
she had with Maury. She expressed a wish to share her
awareness with others. During grief counseling, she went
to see a psychiatrist. She expressed her insights, "I don't
want to be challenged. I don't want to be a better person.
I don't want to learn how to cope with challenges. I
don't want to participate in other people's drama. I don't
have the strength for it at this time. I've got too much
on my plate. I have become much more understanding
of my own limitations and trying to respect them as
opposed to challenging myself. It's enabled me to not do
drama anymore. If someone is upset with me, I tell him
or her, it's your drama. I don't let people put their drama
into my life."

Dolores doesn't think she will have a relationship with a
man at this point in her life. She says, "It would have to be
a very unusual person. Even if it were a possibility, I'm not
willing to do what would be required. I'm not willing to

take on someone's peccadillos or even care whether I'm making someone happy."

Dolores acknowledges we all have a need for connection. She mentions, "There are a group of women I paint with. I never started painting until Maury died. There were parts of myself I put away. I don't know why. I began to realize about two years after he died, there were serious problems with our marriage. My focus during the marriage was keeping the marriage together. So I didn't bring up things. I consciously made the decision not to. When I would become upset about things that were going unresolved, I would get it out in a notebook. Even though I was unforgiving about some things he had done, I was not going to have a broken family. I didn't deal with it, and in retrospect, I think it was actually the right decision for me. It would have been even a bigger cost if our family had broken up."

The results from infidelity in a marriage are devastating. Dolores remembers, "Maury was involved with someone for a very long time. He was living a double life of which I was not consciously aware. I swear I was not. He lied to me for a very long time, years. It was my life too. That relationship ended. He got honest. But there was no awareness of my life. It was like he walked out the door and then walked back in again without any awareness that my life had been going on during this time. Everyone leaves a mixed legacy. I'd take him back in a second. When you really love someone, you love him or her as much for their brokenness as their wholeness. I think he split himself in half- two persons. When I finally asked him how long the affair had been going on, he told me months and months. The story was a long time coming out. They had a place together. There was a violation, but I'm not so sure marriage isn't an arena for these things to happen. People struggle in marriage. It can be very lonely. I think Maury was very ambivalent in his feelings toward women. He was very narcissistic; I said that to him."

Narcissistic people often have a need to make the other person responsible. When he tried to pin it on Dolores, she pointed out, "Maury, once you're off the reservation, you can't blame it on me. I would have tried to work on anything if I had known, but once off the reservation, no way you can pin it on me."

Dolores has a philosophy about marriage. She feels, in some ways, it's totally unnatural, but it's not neutral. She points out up until recently, marriage was based on people in the same community coming together, working on things together for pragmatic reasons. Now, she believes, marriage is based on fulfilling another person, "You fulfill me, and I'll fulfill you. If someone is not faithful, you've failed at fulfilling him or her; they have to go to another person. What is that? Actually, basing a marriage on whether you're being fulfilled and happy, is building a marriage on a very shaky foundation. People need to thrive. If you want to stay in a marriage, you need to be committed to staying in the marriage, not being happy. Finding those things in the context of marriage is too much to ask of another person. Maury, not feeling fulfilled, went to someone else; this wasn't his first marriage. He cheated on her too. If someone comes onto you and you want to get into bed with another person, you're going to look for a thousand reasons to do it. It's human. How the next generation is going to preserve marriage is beyond me. In ours, no one got a divorce; now these kids are growing up in a different world. When marriage was first invented, one of the people might be dead within ten years. Things had not been dealt with in our marriage and coming into resolution about it was very painful. But, it was part of the grieving process. Maury was my hot water bottle. He provided the physical comfort of just being touched. So much has fallen away in this painful process. I have moved into acceptance."

Dolores's life today is full of physical pain. She notes, "I focus on what I need to do today. If I do that, I usually have enough energy. My physical limitations don't give me much choice. So, a lot of my decisions are just based on my limitations. I am physically and emotionally fragile. The sense of protection is lost when women lose husbands. An example of this occurred with my gentleman friend. He was married to my cousin. He is 85, and while driving, he said ugly things about my children. I didn't respond. I didn't want to have this conversation. I became depressed. I couldn't sleep. If my husband had been alive, he would never have opened his mouth to me. A woman alone is vulnerable."

Dolores has become very honest about her life. She observes, "People like drama. You get to the point you don't like it anymore. Drama is a choice. I don't have a choice. You have to be in touch with your own body, physically and emotionally. I don't have resilience at this point. And I don't want to grow another tumor. It's bullshit you have to have the right attitude. Just be positive people say. That denies the truth of your experience. Sometimes you're desolate. People say things that aren't helpful because they're uncomfortable with dark emotions. They don't want to be around difficult situations. You have to be able to recognize drama. When you're involved with drama, you don't even see it."

Dolores has learned to deal with the fact that her relationships with people have changed. She firmly states that, in her experience, there is no such thing as closure. She wishes the term would be taken out of language altogether. She thinks it a ridiculous concept. She acknowledges, "Certainly, time can be helpful. But, you are forever changed by a loss."

As Dolores began to bring forth the parts of herself she had put away, her emotional well-being improved. Whether her views about marriage are ones to agree with or not, they are what sustained her in her life. She said, "Human beings are not designed to walk through this world alone." We are made for relationship. I learned later that the women who painted every week with her made her feel more connected. She began to come out of her emotional isolation. The paintings themselves made her feel more alive.

CHAPTER 9
Spiritual and Soul Relationships

In relationship, we may initially fail to recognize that what we are yearning for is a relationship above the level of human connection. We move into sacred space when we bring the Creator into the dating equation and begin to create together. If we're very lucky, this equation will include God, self, and other.

John Hudak, Director of Community Counseling, brings Christianity into the dating equation. He maintains in order to be successful with any future relationship after loss, you need to go deep within yourself, connect to God, and then your success rate might improve. Whether dating or in any type of connection you make, being a loving, growing person is what you want to do. Human connection is what we want, connection to self, God, and others.

The Ben and Laura Story

Christian dating that leads to a successful commitment is very much present in the story of Ben and Laura. Ben tells that early in their marriage, his wife struggled with infidelity but through perseverance and wanting to keep his family together, they never separated but were eventually restored and enjoyed another 10 years together.

Meanwhile, Laura, who was significantly younger than Ben, is struggling with her own marriage. Her husband and father of their two children didn't want to seek counseling for their differences. Laura set out to get counseling on her own. She went to a Christian counselor but didn't receive the help she needed. Laura said, "Not all Christian counseling lives up to its name, and without any biblical guidance, this didn't lead me toward reconciliation." There was no infidelity, but lots of problems. Laura used the term "death without the casserole" to describe divorce. She says, "You go through the same loss, the brokenness, but divorce isn't treated with the same empathy, in fact, sometimes you are shunned. You can lose friends who don't want to take sides."

Laura and Ben's paths crossed. Ben remembers, "Laura and I went to the same church before our divorces. She was in a class with my wife. As a member of the Board of Elders, I was told Laura and her husband wanted a divorce. I approached her and tried to talk her out of getting a divorce. I told her if my own marriage could get through infidelity, perhaps she and her husband could figure out a way to make it work. I made her cry."

Not too long after this, Ben's wife had a second affair. They decided to end their marriage. "Later, Laura and I were at a church picnic. I approached Laura and said I needed to tell her that I had since got a divorce. We talked and talked."

Laura said Ben had felt the need to tell her since he had counseled her not to get a divorce earlier.

Ben continued, "So we sat on a park bench and talked and talked and talked. The more we talked, the more we found we had things in common. We enjoyed doing the same things. We went to the same church. We both like outdoor things. I like to camp and fish. We were compatible. I was attracted to her. She was cute!"

There is a significant age difference between Ben and Laura, but Laura observes, "That has not been an issue for us in terms of just doing life. It's almost not there. The funniest thing is that Ben would know the words to songs. He would be singing them, and I didn't know the words to songs he would be singing. We were from different generations. He knew my songs, but I didn't know his because his kids sang the songs from my generation. We have so much in common that the age difference is not an issue, and Ben is very youthful.

Laura recalls something that happened to her when she was trying to fix her first marriage. She remembers, " I felt divorce was so wrong. I was so frustrated. I felt like a failure as a wife and a believer. I was hurt and mad, fussing at God." I said to him, "If you would give me a Christian husband, I could be a Christian wife!" Later, when she and Ben were married, they were going through a really rough time. They were arguing about something really big. She remembers that God said to her in her spirit, "I've given you a Christian husband."

That was a foundational turning point in their marriage. Laura observes, "We were both so determined. We were not going to let our marriage be lost. We were so determined to fight for it because we had already had that experience. It's about grit, about sticking with it no matter what. It's about unconditional love. Ben and I sort of came to Jesus together even though we were both a part of our church."

There were issues with Ben's oldest daughter. The night before their wedding, she called Ben and said she couldn't do it-go to their wedding. Ben said, "I understand. I'm sorry you're not going to be there, but you have to do what you have to do." She did end up coming to the wedding. Now, Laura observes, "We are the closest. We are very similar. She has told me twice she was so glad we met and married. That has been a blessing."

Laura's boys accepted Ben. Laura remembers, "They wanted us to be a family. I wanted Ben to love my kids the way I loved them. It was a very hard reality for me to accept that he could never love them the way I loved them, the way he loves his own. It's not that he doesn't love my children; he cares very much for them. We all give our own kids more of an advantage.

We are able to include my ex-husband and his wife in some of our family outings. My children really enjoy having their dad and his wife sitting around the campfire together with us." Laura credits forgiveness for this.

But Laura also notes, "Forgiveness is not a feeling; it's a decision. God is a great forgiver; we cannot do less."

Laura does admit the difference in their ages has become more pronounced than it was when they first got married. She observes, "He's had cancer twice, prostate and throat cancer. It is a factor. As he ages, I don't expect that to change. Our marriage has gotten better and better. There is more love than ten years ago. But it's harder now, more imminent. Maybe I'm going to be okay. It's going to look different. Maybe I'm going to be up to it. If I look at the times in my life when I've been fearful, He's provided."

The stories in this chapter tell of couples that agreed consciously to place God at the center of their relationship. Their conscious quest was to seek out a person who loves God and go from there. The following story points out that struggle and loss are a part of the life of faith.

The Doug and Nan Story

Doug was married in 1967 to a student teacher in the school where he was teaching. They married; she became a teacher; Doug was a coach at this time. Doug remembers, "I coached 7-8 years. I left the teaching profession; she got breast cancer. We were married 18 years and had two children, both boys."

Nan's marital history is very different. She married twice. Nan recalls, "I was married very young while I was in high school when I became pregnant. He was an alcoholic, a druggie, very abusive." They were married six years. When her daughter was five years old, I just said to myself, "I'm out of here."

Nan was clear about her intentions, "I wanted to become a teacher to help teenagers make better decisions than I made, get more guidance than I got."

Nan came to the university in 1969. She filed for divorce, and it went through uncontested. She said, "I met a young man from a German family. He was just out of the Navy, a good person, just not the right person for me to marry. He was very controlling, although not abusive. We came from different backgrounds. His family was very judgmental, especially of Black people, and my brother had married a Black girl. He discovered I had invited my brother to our wedding. As I watched the little girls go before me down the aisle, I said to my Father, I think I might be making a mistake."

My Dad said to me, "Then we'll just walk back out."

Nan replied, "No, I can't do that." So she married him.
They worked at it for a long time. Finally, Nan said, "I
can't do this anymore. But, I never knew when to quit.
The time came when I was coming home from play
practice. I stopped at a four-way stop. I, literally, didn't
know where to go next with my life. I became ill. I was
hospitalized 4-5 days. The doctor advised me this was all
about stress. After tests, he told me I was going to have to
do something."

Nan continued, "We were divorced after 12 years in the
marriage. Yes, there had been red flags from the beginning.
My daughter who had been five at the time of our
marriage was always a high maintenance kid. She did not
want me to marry him. She did not like him. She did not
want him to be her disciplinarian. We went to counseling
about that. We divorced in '84-'85."

Experts would classify this relationship as a transitional
one. " If you try to have a romantic relationship meet
your needs for healing, it is not going to work. You need
a support system to ground you so that you can make
choices out of strength," according to Drs. Cloud and
Townsend, the authors of Boundaries in Dating (74).
Nan recalls she met Doug in 1991 after being divorced
in 1985. "We actually lived three houses away from each
other, but we didn't know each other."

According to Doug, "Nan graduated from college with my
wife. I met Nan a year after my wife died."

"God took care of that," Nan interjected. "I taught high
school speech and debate. When we would go to meets,
my girls would go around and check out all the coaches
to see who wasn't married. They would come back and

report which coaches were single and tell me I needed to meet them. Tabitha was a student I was close to. She worked for Doug in his convenience store. In April, the yearbooks came out. Tabitha took the yearbook to work and asked Doug if he was dating. He said no, so she asked him to take a look at the teachers to determine if there were ones he would be inclined to date. He picked two of them and one was me."

There was another young girl living with Nan at the time going to school. She and Tabitha cooked up a scheme whereby they would take Nan and stop by Doug's store for coffee. Tabitha said, "My boss really wants to meet you." So the three of them went for coffee, but Doug wasn't there. "You can't just leave!" Tabitha gave Nan a post-it note telling her to leave her phone number with a message to call her.

When Nan arrived home a couple of days later, there were signs all over saying, "He called, he called, he called." Nan tells, "I called him back and he came over for coffee. But I made it clear saying, I just want you to know up front, this isn't going anywhere. It would be nice to have a friend to go with to the boys' games, but that's all."

Doug explained, "Even though Nan told me she needed me to understand this was not a serious relationship, that didn't last very long. A year later, we were married."

Recalling that Nan's dad was part Cherokee Indian, Doug approached her Dad to ask him for Nan's hand in marriage. Her dad said, "She's old, she's been used, the price is ten horses." Doug brought him ten little plastic horses. He said, "I'm going to buy your daughter." Her dad walked out, got into the sandbox and started playing with the grandchildren. He didn't say a word. "I got him," Doug said.

With three teenagers all approximately the same age, Doug explained how they made it work, "I didn't discipline hers; she didn't discipline mine. My oldest son said he wouldn't live with another woman, not his Mother. I told him I guess you're going to have to find a place to live then, because we're going to get married." Nan observed that he was still grieving for his Mother. Doug notes that today, his son is her greatest ally.

Nan interrupted, "If I had known he had these adamant objections, I would never have married Doug because I had been through my own daughter's objections to my second marriage. Nan calls it a God thing, "Our whole marriage has been a God thing because how many people can put three teenage boys together and make it work?"

I asked Doug how he set boundaries about dealing with differences? He quipped, "I just always say yes to her." It was, of course, not that simple. Nan said, "It takes a lot of compromise, but one thing Doug and I probably didn't think through was how different we are. I said, God you did this thing so you just work this mess out. Doug is a sports person. He loves golf and golf stores. I love sewing, going to plays, garage sales and antique stores."

One of the times Nan became emotional was describing the crises that beset their lives for a time. "My dad died one year after our marriage in a freak accident. Shortly after that, my Mother had to have back surgery. Both of Doug's brothers were in the hospital and nearly died. Shortly after my grandson's birth, my daughter had to go into drug and alcohol rehab. We took the little boy. It was one thing after another. My mother was very ill; she was on life support for 35 days. My youngest brother suffered a heart attack. Within a year, my Grandmother, the one who had helped me go to school, died, and then my brother died. My step dad died. Then Doug got Cancer in '09. There was a period of years when we suffered trauma upon trauma, one thing after another. No time for recovery between events. I don't know if we would know how to deal with a year of no…" "Conflict," Doug finished her sentence. They were completely dependent on each other.

Nan said, "The crises always brought us together. There wasn't a time when he wasn't there holding my hand. So Doug and I learned how to be okay with differences. We grew closer. My Mom was not going to make it. We would lie in bed at night holding hands and repeating together the 23rd Psalm. "

Now Nan and Doug are dealing with retirement, another adjustment. It is clear, however, they are dealing with it by honoring the boundaries that keep them together, but separate. Doug has his activities, and Nan has hers, but they continue to function as a unit. Through Nan and Doug's story, it is clear that Christ dwells in their relationship.

CHAPTER 10
I Don't Look Good Naked
Anymore

The Don Story

What constitutes sex especially among seniors is a subject many seniors themselves have differing opinions about. Don, an 85-year-old senior, had definite ideas on the subject. Don started dating about six to eight months following his wife's death. He reflects, "I was looking for companionship, but eventually, sex became my major goal. I would not be attracted to a woman who had not taken care of herself. No matter what her age, a woman would have to be in good physical shape for me to be attracted to her."

Don swims, exercises regularly, and makes no bones that aging bodies not withstanding, he is selective about appearances. Although he estimates he has taken about ten women to church or other senior activities connected to the center where he resides , he states, "I did not form lasting unions with any of those women except for one because most of those women did not fit into the category I wanted."

There was only one woman he pursued with vigor. She was attractive, and he let her know what he was interested in. Don reports, "She would say on occasion that I need to find a younger woman, but I don't think she means it. I think there would be jealousy involved if either of us strayed to other people very often. I think that's only natural. The relationship probably needs to be exclusive in the long run."

This exclusive relationship pattern seems to be favored by most seniors. Typically, they pair off. Research shows if they are going to date more than one person at a time, they need to be transparent.

Don openly says he has been successful with sex being his primary goal in the relationship he pursued. Don admits, "Broad definitions of what constitutes sex are out there, but that is normally not what a man is looking for. For me, penetration is required."

He admits that he has also lost a relationship over boundaries a woman has set. He smiles and states, "About 15 times, I have been dumped by the same woman. We would negotiate this issue, but it kept returning. I am not having sex at the present time, so I guess she won the boundary battle. Regrettably, this part of our relationship never returned to the stage it was at before. Once you are lovers, it is hard to give it up."

As to the future, Don says, "I am still traveling and want to travel. When traveling with a woman, her desiring her own stateroom is not a deal breaker. However, at some stage, that has got to change. I've traveled with a couple of women who've had their own room, and me mine. Although, I believe that most men would be willing to travel separately, there has to be some chemistry. With chemistry, sex may follow."

Whether Don's perception of what constitutes sex is accurate, what is clear is that senior sex is here to stay. In retirement communities all over the country, there are reports of rapid increases in S. T. D.'s among older people. In the article, Sex and the Single Senior, Ezekiel J. Emanuel reports that "between 2007 and 2011, chlamydia infections among Americans 65 and over increased by 31 percent, and syphilis by 52 percent. Those numbers are similar to S. T. D. trends in the 20-to 24-year-old age group."

There are several reasons for this. Seniors are living together in close proximity more than ever, and things are going to happen. Nurses in these facilities where residents must report their medications say that every year, the number of prescriptions written for a new class of medications including Viagra are increasing. It's a fact that older Americans are continuing to enjoy an active sex life.

Getting away from the scholarly facts, there is no replacement for human contact. People like to feel alive, and one way to do this is through being close to somebody. The following story demonstrates that seniors may benefit from looking at creative ways to be sexual.

The Louis and Carolyn Story

Carolyn believed there were many ways to be intimate. When she met Louis, it was just a case of poor timing. If they had met even 10 years ago when Louis would have been 75 and Carolyn 60, perhaps intimate relations would not have been so problematic.

Fate had brought them together at a point in their lives when neither had been sexually active for at least 25 years. With Louis, his wife, the love of his life, had stopped recognizing him as her husband. Dementia had stolen her memory of him. He discovered after her death that at one point, she had written in her journal that her "father" had driven her on errands. That discovery partially explained why she had avoided intimacy early on.

With Carolyn, her husband's increasing health issues had brought an end to the sexual activity in her marriage when she was no more than 50. In short, they were both out of practice. The cruel irony was that in the present, Carolyn and Louis were now free to become intimate, but there were age related issues.

A few months into their dating relationship, it became clear there was chemistry. Through touching, latent sexuality was rekindled. It became clear, time and aging had wrought changes. Help was needed. Louis was willing to have the conversation with his primary care physician about whether he was healthy enough to have sex. He was.

Carolyn was concerned gravity and time had wrought changes in her body. Louis assured Carolyn her body was beautiful to him. There was not an expectation of perfection. When kissing and touching were not enough, it was time for Louis to swallow a pill and see what happened. What happened was spectacular.

The Levitra was only partially successful. Carolyn gravitated toward helping with the process. Louis, instinctively, began running his fingers through her hair. Who knew the nerve endings in the scalp could heighten sensitivity? Soon, they were bathed in mega doses of oxytocin. New ways of experimenting with the power of touch were born.

Soon, the couple was engaged in trailblazing discoveries involving the particularly sensitive areas of the body other than primary sexual organs, which can fail. The bottoms of the feet are the source of more than 11,000 nerve endings. The ears are particularly sensitive, especially the insides. A little known fact they discovered is that touching the inside of the navel can be erotic. Stimulating the nerves in the sensitive areas gives a jolt of the mood-boosting neurotransmitter serotonin.

In this way seniors can be sexually active much later in life. Several major surveys report that among people age 60 and older, more than half of men and 40 percent of women continue to be sexually active. We just need to be creative.

CHAPTER 11
Connected Forever

When we are living in harmony with ourselves rather than as a prisoner of societal imperatives, we can embrace relationships based on love, cooperation, and communication. This may or may not involve marriage.

The Jim and Julie Story

Jim and Julie seem to have a very successful relationship. They bought a house together and have lived together the last 3-4 years. They choose not to marry. Jim made contact with Julie on December 4, 2011 after 25 years. They saw each other in person by Christmas. Sometimes, it seems, people are fated to come together. Such seems to be the case with Jim and Julie.

Jim recalls, "I was married when I was 35, and remained married for 22 years. We had two children, both boys, but it was mostly pretty sad. I am still finding words. We had a lot of incompleteness, a lot of loss. Actually, one of the unspoken bonds was loss. There were bonds of misery. I believe it's possible for lovers to enrich each other. It helps you to grow. I wanted that in that marriage. It was very hard for me to let go that dream. It caused more suffering than was necessary. I accepted a lot of criticism, a lot of misery. Even though I didn't like it, I was powerfully conditioned to accept it as part of my life. I didn't have great models for relationship."

Julie was married very young at 20. She had two children at age 21 and 23. She got ovarian cancer at age 24. She had married to get out of the house where she grew up as it was not a pleasant place to be. During her bout with cancer, the marriage started breaking up. She remembers, "As a child, I loved horses. During the marriage, my

husband was on the corporate track. He was involved with
the country club. I loved riding horses. It was starting
to ground me. I was finding out who I was. I was a late
bloomer. The horses were helping. I was not comfortable
being a corporate wife. I felt part of the furniture that
made him look good. I was an extension of him, arm
candy. I wouldn't go to the country club. I grew up with
a lot of anger in my family. If you haven't solved it in
yourself, it continues to show up. My husband was very
angry, abusive really. We built a barn for the horses, that's
how I met Jim, way, way back. I didn't know how to talk
to men, but Jim and I started talking. I opened up ideas
and thoughts. One of them was I couldn't stay married
anymore. I'm not the person my husband thought I was.
He didn't know me. The very beginning of my opening up
came with Jim."

At the end of Jim's marriage there was a tremendous
yearning for connection. His ex could not carry on
a conversation. "There was no give and take. It was
extremely frustrating. I had a yearning for female
companionship. It was not sexual; I just wanted to talk. My
own experience was so miserable. I reached out to women
I'd known before I got married. Julie had cancer. I began
to think, I've got to talk with Julie. I don't care if I have to
share her with someone. I don't even know if she's alive. I
just need to talk to her."

Julie explained those conversations happened before Jim
met his wife. She remembers, "Jim and I lived together for
a while. The baggage we brought to the relationship did
not allow us to stay together. It was very painful for me
and still is in some ways. We were both heartbroken." Julie
says her baggage came mostly from an inability to speak
from an authentic place in her. She says, "It would have

been much too vulnerable for me to let him know how deeply I loved him."

Jim said, "It was a marvelous time in my life I never had that degree of intimacy, never felt that secure. There was a tremendous amount riding on my relationship with Julie. It represented a lot of hope. We both had dismal previous relationships especially with family members,and choices of partners. We had desolate relationships with parents and siblings. There was an affirmation with Julie of a loving, intelligent connection.

Julie said they couldn't talk about issues. She recalls, "My children were not happy with Jim in the role of their father." The daughters said, "Mama, you should try harder." Julie finally began to realize why she was not with their father.

She acknowledges, "Even now, my daughters are not thrilled with me being with Jim. It has caused a rift. My older daughter is not talking to me. When my younger daughter learned the two of us were together, she said to me in a phone conversation, "Have you no shame?"

Julie admits it's partly my fault. She recalls, "During the years after Jim and I broke up, I was pretty raw. I did not parent them well during that difficult time. During the tender years of their adolescence, no good parenting came from either parent. My sister was afraid I was going to get hurt again. I started back to college and got a social work degree. There was no good safety network during these difficult years. Jim and I had no contact for 25 years. I had a couple of long term relationships, but Jim was the benchmark. They couldn't measure up. We'd shared each other's growth. They weren't terrible people, but I was constantly disappointed. All those years, he was in my heart. I heard he got married, and I was not going to pursue him."

Jim says, "I never stopped thinking about Julie." Constantly, other women reminded me of her. All I could see was Julie. When we look at photos, I'm supposed to be there. Where was I?"

Julie had moved to North Carolina. She recalls a pivotal moment, "on December 4, 2011, I was checking my e-mail. There was one from Jim. This was our first contact after all the years of separation. It read, 'Are you okay?' This was a tremendously dramatic moment. I could hardly breathe! The world stopped. I was afraid to return contact. I was neutral in my response because of past hurt. I felt the floor open up. We wrote long e-mails to each other the whole month of December. Our writings from then were beautiful."

The problem then was proximity. Julie had been living in Ashville, North Carolina for about eight years. Her kids were long gone. Jim knew he could not live in North Carolina. He was still going through his divorce. He recalls, "I was waiting for my kids to grow up. My ex-wife was holding my kids captive. I needed to be available for when the poison wore off. My work is in Rochester. My customer base is here. Financially, I was in terrible shape. My ex didn't want to work. I was never in a position to be a big earner. I'm in a traditional craft. My kids have large medical needs. My youngest has been diabetic since the age of eight. My oldest was diagnosed with Asperger's." There were many challenges facing Julie and Jim.

Not the least of these challenges was dealing with what everyone thought about Julie and Jim getting back together. The woman who kept Julie's horse commented, "Julie would live on a rock if that's where Jim was."

Jim notes that Julie was different this time. "She had a lovely voice when writing to me. When we got together, I noticed she was not hiding her intelligence." Julie explains she was not quite claiming it before. "I didn't think I was very smart. My father discouraged it. He didn't want me to try to be a veterinarian. He thought I should be a support person."

Julie and Jim have common interests. Julie recalls, Jim opened up canoe camping to me before. When we were young, he taught me how to canoe in the wilderness. When we broke up, I took solo trips and learned how capable I was. We enjoy music of all sorts. We enjoy ideas, talking to each other. We talk in the mornings. Jim often would be late to work with our talking. Our sleep patterns became taking 4-5 hours to sleep, waking up then to talk. We were making up for lost time."

Julie describes working hard physically in the years before she got back together with Jim. "Part of the appeal was to manage powerful feelings I carried around. Both of us grew up in families that were impossible. We never got a chance to be who we were. That conditioning never allowed us to love and feel loved."

Jim reflects, "I had to go through the crucible of bad choices to learn how to retrieve who I thought I could be. Maturity has helped. You have to go through it. During my whole married life, the benchmark with Julie was alive in me, but I hung on for a long time because I was afraid of the vulnerability of my kids. The last three years with Julie have been the period of most growth in myself. There are other factors, but having Julie in my life and giving love has allowed me to mature in ways I never had before. The invitation exists to grow. As each one of us moves forward, it raises anxiety, but we're okay with it. We might have scared each other at first, but the strong bottom line is being well loved and being able to receive the love that is offered. The old me couldn't take it in very well. As I receive, there's more I can put out. This continues to feed us."

The Katie and Ken Story

Sometimes fate steps in and intervenes in the lives of humans. Such was the case with Katie and Ken. Late in both their lives Katie and Ken came together in a great relationship.

Recently, when Katie entered my home for our interview, she was an imposing figure, still lovely. Nearly six feet tall, despite her age of 89 years, she was statuesque and regally clad in a fashionable outfit complete with tasteful jewelry. The southern accent was still apparent. She was articulate in telling their story.

For many years, Katie and Ken resided within side-by-side homes in the estate section of a senior living center. They knew each other, but just as neighbors. Eventually, Katie's husband of many years passed away. Katie mourned, but rebuilt her life with family, friends, and varied activities. It seemed Katie was destined to remain a widow. Many years went by, but like many resilient people, Katie's life was full, and she was not looking for another relationship. She was in her eighties.

In 2009, Ken's wife passed away after a cancer that took her quickly. Ken's youngest daughter, remembering her mother, said, "My mom was one of the most inclusive people I have ever known. She never met a stranger, always positive. I never heard her say a bad word about anybody. She is the main reason we kids are so inclusive about Katie. Mom taught us that. Mom included everyone whether she knew him or her or not. She was happy to meet new people. Mom taught us to include others. Through her legacy, I knew I needed to have that positive outlook as well. "

"Dad was more stoic, quiet. When Mom died, Dad knew he needed to step up, so he became more inclusive, but it was more difficult for him, not natural as it was for Mom."

During Mom's funeral service, the pastor said, "The church has lost some of its joy"

"Who is going to step up to fill that void?" Tammy's sister said. "Mom is the reason we are the way we are."

Tammy says, "Dad was my rock. I was his and he was mine. But Mom taught us how to love."

As the story of Katie and Ken's relationship unfolded, I was to see that Tammy's support of their relationship was unique. Many adult daughters have an issue with seeing their father develop a connection with another woman. Not so with Tammy.. Tammy has a strong character and was generous sharing her father with Katie. Tammy had seen that her father was bereft following the loss of his wife. Tammy observed her father not functioning well. He was very lonely.

Katie was active socially remaining connected to both married friends and other widows. There came a time when a group of friends began to go to dinner every Thursday. Serendipity descended, and Ken ended up her dinner partner. They were able to eat with each other in this relaxed atmosphere with others present so that the conversational burden was shared and no awkward first date moments occurred.

From that time forward, it appeared their personalities were compatible and they had shared values. In the ensuing weeks, Tammy noticed that her dad's demeanor changed. He stood up straighter, was more animated, and the fog that had surrounded him was lifting. From the beginning of Katie and Ken's relationship, Tammy was around. She worked not far away, and it was her habit to spend her lunch hour with Ken. She observed the positive changes in her father as he got to know Katie.

Fortunately, Katie and Ken were in reasonably good health at this time. They were active and mobile. They were both still driving. They began to go places together. Most times Ken drove, but sometimes, Katie.

Humor was a part of their connection. They went to different churches, but on one occasion, Ken took Katie to a funeral at his church. The next day as they were running errands, Katie drove. One of her errands was to drop off cleaning nearby. She quipped, "He took me to church, and I took him to the cleaners."

Tammy recalls that her dad was fascinated with Katie's unique Southern pronunciation. Katie decided Ken's front door need sprucing up, so she prepared a wreath for his door. She referred to it as a "reef". Ken called these "Katieisms".

In her younger years, Katie was an avid gardener. Aging took its toll on her ability to be active in her garden. She missed it. One day, she was out with her flowers working away when she lost her balance. She fell and was unable to get herself up. Wisely, she had her cellphone with her, and she called Ken to assist her. Always the provider, he hastened over to get her up. In so doing, he lost his balance, and fell on the concrete. Katie joked, "He really fell hard for me."

They were already companions, but neither felt the need to marry. Their financial situations were complicated. Both had large families which made merging the family structure formidable. But Katie says the main reason is they just didn't feel the need. Their proximity to each other facilitated access. There was just nothing missing from their relationship.

As they became more comfortable with each other, they began to talk on the phone regularly. Katie liked to cook, and Ken didn't, so mealtimes were sometimes shared. One evening, Katie was enjoying sitting outside, but wanted Ken to share the out-of-doors with her. When she called to invite him over, Ken stated he was already in his nightclothes. But he decided he could slip across the space between their backyards and join Katie.

Ken was a gentleman, though, and was careful with appearances. One evening, as he was delivering Katie home, she noticed that he wasn't driving away after dropping her off. Ken said his car wouldn't start. He was agitated about having to leave his car in Katie's driveway overnight until assistance could be summoned the next morning. He wanted to protect Katie's reputation.

They did travel together on a couple of occasions, once to visit his family, staying overnight. Tammy accompanied them on that trip. There was another occasion where Ken escorted Katie to visit her family.

Tammy said merging their families was never awkward. She remembered a couple of holidays in which Katie would join their family group if hers were not available. Tammy was used to trusting her father's judgment. She could see that Katie enhanced her father's life.

There came a time during the five years Katie and Ken shared when Ken fell and broke his hip. This required rehabilitation in the health center part of their senior living facility. Katie came every day to be with Ken. Tammy noticed that the moment Katie walked into his room, Ken's eyes lit up.

Ken was shuffling before he fell, but when Katie summoned Ken to walk upright with a healthy gait, he always made an effort. Katie would say, "stride, Ken, stride!" He clearly wanted to please Katie. Ken never walked after he broke his hip.

Katie and Ken had a unique way of balancing dating and still managing to retain the freedom of who they were. They managed to stay separate while coming together often. Although there was a lot of give and take, neither compromised their lifestyle and interests for the sake of the relationship.

In an effort to share Ken's love of music, Katie undertook to play the piano. With Ken's encouragement, she came to the point of being ready to perform a duet on the piano with Ken, a simple song, "Tea For Two." Although she labored mightily, it soon became clear, she lacked Ken's talent.

Katie's love was playing bridge, and she was very good at it. In an effort to please Katie, Ken laboriously undertook learning to play bridge. Although he could never give up his "cheat sheet" set of hints on how to proceed, he gave it his best shot. After a time, he communicated to Katie that bridge was never going to be his game, and he just wasn't into it. They settled on that Katie would be the bridge player, and Ken would focus on his music. Wisely, neither tried to change who the other was.

Katie remembers that she and Ken enjoyed doing simple things together. They liked to go to the riverfront and sit on a bench and be still together. They often went to get ice cream in the summer or to an event at the River Campus. Their connection grew during the years they had together.

They were great companions; they cared a lot for each other. Fate may have brought them together, but as is often the case, it was for a season. Tammy tells of how her family included Katie when the time came for Ken's life to slip away.

Tammy's brother prepared a eulogy for his dad's services in which he made a tribute to Katie and her connection to his father. Katie sat with the family, and her name was prominent when Ken's obituary was published referring to Katie as Ken's companion and friend.

After Ken's death, Tammy took Katie to breakfast most Saturday mornings, up until the last week of Katie's life. They shared a remarkable relationship. As this book went to press, the family reports that Katie passed away at the age of 90. She would have wanted her story to be told.

CHAPTER 12
Self Awareness

The Naomi Story

Naomi's story of relationships will inspire others who have struggled. Naomi learned well that after loss, one needs to take time out to journey within, find the source of his or her own strength, learn to enjoy his or her own company and give love to oneself.

Naomi recalls, "In 1994, I made the decision to embark on a further course of study. My marriage was already in trouble and going to a distant land with my two children was a way of escape for me. I was married to a high profile lawyer who as a husband was verbally, physically, emotionally and financially abusive. Through workshops on psychotherapy that I enrolled in as part of my course work, I soon realized that I was in a difficult situation that I needed to do something about. I remember how at the end of the workshop, there was a requirement to write a professional empowerment piece. I veered off and wrote about my painful relationship with my then husband. Fortunate enough for me, my deep cries for help were deeply felt and I received the professional help I needed.

I recall how later, when I travelled back home to re-unite with my husband, the relationship was dead. Neither of us established eye contact. I had outgrown the relationship given the confident woman I had become. I was ready to face whatever difficulty life presented me with in pursuit of a new life for myself. My children were grown, and had a voice. They could speak their minds. I decided to pursue the divorce.

My husband was a prominent and popular lawyer. When I married him, I was a young girl, ten years younger than him. Everybody would ask him; 'Where did you find her?' That was great for his ego. Meanwhile behind closed doors, he was abusing me. I was just a piece of something to complete his picture as a complete man. I decided to have none of it. The divorce came through after two long, tedious years. The reality was devastating.

There is as much loss with divorce as there is with death [sometimes more]. In the community that I lived in at the time, divorce is fiercely frowned upon and despised. Failure of a marriage is the woman's fault because women are expected to withstand all hardships that come with marital life, abuse included. It came as no surprise although hurtful, that society gradually pushed me aside and alienated me. I was used to being around very prominent people in society, I suddenly lost that. I was living a prestigious life, lived in a posh suburb, big house and nice neighborhood but soon lost all that. I lost everything that came with the status of being married. I lost close friends who were associated with the marriage. Men didn't want their wives to be around me and get ideas about divorcing them. So I found myself alone, having to start life afresh with new people because people perceived me differently."

Naomi said she was a person of deep faith and didn't want to have a relationship just for the sake of having one. "I told God, 'You are going to be my relationship until I figure things out. If you give me someone, I will take him, but I am not looking for a relationship.' I wanted a relationship with myself. I wanted to fully know me. I was born of parents who were of the Christian faith. I was brought up going to Church. I depended on my faith. It's always been a part of me. So when things go wrong I go to my source, to God and cry out for Him to direct me, show me, and lead me where I should go. I embarked on a self-discovery journey. I recall talking to myself about how I had never experienced living independently, on my own. I went from my father's house straight into marital life, into another man's house. I never learned my strengths, my likes, my habits and who I really was. I decided, this was time for me to know me. I read a lot of self-development literature. I read about relationships, good and bad. I started enjoying watching movies. I was happy but at the same time allowed myself time to experience the loss and grieve. Eventually, I learned to be with me, with myself, and enjoy myself. I learned to be enough and content by myself. I did not need another person to make me happy. If Naomi could not provide for Naomi, why would I expect someone to do it for me? For a long, long time, I wasn't thinking about a man."

"I'm not going to lie and say I was completely uninvolved with men. There were plenty of guys who would approach me, but all they wanted was to sleep with me. I could see through them. I didn't want a superficial relationship. I wanted a relationship with someone who was emotionally mature and confident. Strangely, most of the men were married. I asked them, 'why are you doing that?' That is what I had gotten out of, someone who would lie to me. I didn't want those kinds of relationships."

Naomi's next relationship didn't work out either. She recalls, "In 2008, I met a man at an Independence Celebration party. We spoke briefly, before departing to our respective states. I made nothing of the meeting at the time. We connected via email once we were back home. Emails became phone calls. Phone calls became skype calls and we would spend hours talking. After two years, we decided to get married. It was an exciting wedding and we did enjoy some exciting moments together.

At the time we got married, I was on the dissertation phase of my PhD program and I was also working part-time. I had a lot of work on my hands and time management was very critical for me to meet the strict deadlines and graduate. I thought I had found someone mature, who would be supportive to my pursuits and I would be supportive to his. It was not so. I found myself being the sole bread winner with a man who was not keen on finding a good job and holding it down. He was plain lazy. He didn't want to work. He expected me to take care of him. I told him plainly; 'I am not going to take care of you. You need to get up and do things for yourself.' After a while of Naomi's pushing, he left. Again, Naomi was in devastating shock. Another failure? How could it be? Naomi experienced feelings of rejection, feelings of being taken for a ride. She lost confidence in herself to choose who or what was good for her. It was most embarrassing not to have a marriage relationship last even one year. He was gone before the first wedding anniversary. She thought, 'You fooled me for so long. You made me believe in something for so long. You married me. Why didn't I see through you?' Now she's afraid of trusting her own judgment. She's gone back and forth trying to examine where she went wrong. She thought because they were always on Skype, things were okay. Now she concludes that sustaining a long distance relationship is difficult. Now she thinks you must be with the person, be able to examine them personally.

Naomi still has insecurities about long distance relationships. She ponders, "I'm talking to someone right now. He lives in another country. He tells me that he loved me the first time we met decades back and has never forgotten about me. He married and had three beautiful daughters but ended up in divorce. He pursues me with profound words, texts, e-mails, and phone calls. He has never hesitated about the reason he is pursuing me. He has talked marriage from day one and he keeps telling me he wants to marry me. He doesn't talk about anything else. I keep telling him we have to meet and talk face to face. I am afraid of "Untelling" that I have lost another relationship. The attraction is mutual and strong. It scares me. I never have heard this kind of love language from a man. It's worse when he recounts specific things he remembers about me from way back then. He talks about seeing me in specific situations with detailed descriptions, like a time in the past when I dismissed his advances and told him off quoting my exact words. He reminds me of when, how long and where we worked together. I was never aware of how much I captured his heart and attention way back then. I had no idea of his awareness. He is super intelligent, responsible and very loving to his daughters and I find that super attractive about him. He is very committed and very caring about his girls. He's planning on coming to visit, and I'm confused."

Naomi likes that the man in her new relationship is so respectful. She likes that he honors her. She doesn't want to punish this good man because of how she was treated in the past. The thought of passing up a genuinely good man because of her two painful previous experiences hounds her. Naomi observes, "I like what I see in him. He takes care of himself, cooks, cleans, and does his own laundry. He's an accomplished man. He's not trying to take advantage of me. He doesn't have to. I have come to a point where I say to myself, why do I need a man? If I am going to have a man, he must come to add value, do something I can't do for myself and be my friend, my companion, and my soul mate."

Naomi anticipates the future, "When he comes, I want to see what he is in person compared to what he writes. I am interested to see what the chemistry will be in reality. The chemistry is strong in our writing. Given his presentation right now, I have no reason not to like him. I respect him. He is in awe of what I have accomplished. But is it too good to be true? I am waiting to see.

I definitely entertain thoughts of having this new man in my life because his kindness, disposition and demeanor remind me of my father. I don't know whether I'm confusing the two. My father passed away 15 years ago when he was only 69. That complicates things. He's connected with a spot in my heart that misses my dad. That draws me to him. I feel my father's love when I am with him. It scares me. He's not my father, but there's a connection. I know what kind of relationship my father would want for me. He told me the relationship with my first husband was not going to work. My first husband, according to my father, was an arrogant man. My new person and I are the same age."

Naomi has done the work and still needs to do more because of the two marriages. She is whole and complete and standing on her own two feet. Now she must evaluate how to respond to the situation she confronts in her life.

The Charlotte and Steve Story

Much can be learned from the story of Charlotte and Steve. Charlotte was married young, and the marriage lasted for 17 years. Naively, she thought it would be a forever connection, but that was not to be. It turned out to be a long growing up time. Charlotte described her loss following divorce. "Divorce was like death, but not final. You have to go through a grieving process. You continue on because you still have to have a relationship with that person so that's where forgiveness comes in. It is not something that happens in one day. It's a 70 x 7 process of forgiving, which means it's a continual growth process. I would become very peaceful where I was; then there would be a flair-up, something nostalgic, an event comes up. You have to go through the processing of those emotions and practice forgiveness. I learned a lot about forgiveness through divorce, and that process can be a lot like death except death is final.

When someone dies, and they're gone, you focus on the good of that person. You deal with the memory of that person instead of experiencing day-to-day interactions. With divorce, during the process of forgiving, things flair up again, and emotions come out where with death, it is final. With divorce, you start to look back on the regrets and disappointments, and the 'coulda', 'shoulda' thing prevails. "

Charlotte remembers, "Some even lose friends after divorce. My friends didn't feel they had to choose. It was more of a natural process. With the situation, friends are disappointed. They're going through loss too. What I thought I lost was my identity of being a wife. My role as

151

wife was the center of my relationship. It was my world, and when I started to lose that, it felt like I was losing my sense of worth, and that can be true whether in death or divorce. You had so much wrapped up in your relationship that you thought was your identity: relationships, activities, home, career. When it's gone, you're left with a loss. Who am I now? What do I do? It is helpful to distinguish that identity is different from the role we play in life. I focused on roles that were constantly changing: teacher, wife, and mother. Things were up in the air.

For me, identity is how do I react? How do I live? How do I love? Am I loyal? Do I show up? They're constants. I had to go inside, identify with things that were never going to change. That's where I began to separate roles from identity. "

Charlotte described how she was so wrapped up in her day-to-day world that she thought it defined her. She posed the question, "When that is gone, what do you build on? Certainly, it is disappointing, but when you get through the process, you realize you're in charge of that. Your roles are changing; you can redefine your roles, pick a new role."

For Charlotte, the good news is we get to choose, to decide. "When you give yourself permission to do that, it's another exciting benefit coming through loss. Now I get to choose different roles."

Fortunately, Charlotte had a good listener to talk to. Her counselor had a theology background and could support her in the notion that talking to herself was the same as talking to God. Through him and her own faith, she learned to be constantly in prayer. She explains, "I didn't receive what I received by just the Holy Spirit inside me. There was an ongoing conversation looking for the next step and the next. I didn't react quickly. It was hours of prayer, which isn't traditional prayer. It's conversation with self, talking with God. The Divine guidance she received was the source of spiritual strength. I stayed connected to that voice inside. For me, exercise was another way I talked to God. I got a lot of divine information from exercise. Also, I love Christian music. I walked or ran or listened to the words and music. There was guidance in these activities. They kept me in a state of doing something you love to do. Lose yourself in something that's positive, not in dating to fill a void."

She also learned to seek the attention of others. "Through music, prayer, exercise and friends, it can launch our thoughts in different directions. God was talking to me. This helped with ruminating, where the mind will constantly go over and over something trying to figure it out. You have to break the cycle of grief and loss or you can end up in a state of ruminating. To break the pattern, I use prayer, exercise, music and people. Involving oneself with these things helps to shut the mind down, gaining a new perspective or finding peace. It can calm the ruminating, stop the cycle."

Charlotte learned a lot through her dating experience following loss. "Early on, I dated two or three different gentlemen, nothing serious. I thought I loved these people at different times because I was learning things about myself. I never felt desperation to marry or make a commitment. I did like the connection of being in relationship. It is comforting to us all. When you have that connection for a long time in your life, you miss it. Transitional relationships can and do occur along the way. A lot of women don't know how not to be in a relationship, so they go through the process, not realizing that the relationship has some quirks or faults."

Research shows that second marriages fail at a higher percentage than the first. Charlotte notes, "I did not want to get into that while raising a child. I did not want to put my son into that situation, putting him into a childhood that had some instability due to Mom's relationships. I stayed very focused on parenting him and didn't feel the need to jump in. I'm trying to balance those things in my life that are important to me. I'm learning about that. I could try to please my son until the day I die, and that wouldn't be healthy for me. I get to choose who I want to be and whom I want to be involved with as well. It is an integral part of our day-to-day world,

 What influences me influences my son. It is important to pick the right person especially while everyone is under the same roof. I am cautious about that. My financial independence allows me to do that. Not needing financial support made it easier to do the best I could for my son. It allows me to choose the best for me too."

Charlotte explains that her current serious relationship is with Steve. He was the scoutmaster of her son's pack since second grade. Her current friends were neighbors of Steve's. She connected with a nice group of people. This has allowed Charlotte to be friends with Steve for five years before they formed a dating relationship. The close group of friends enjoyed fun nights. They played together as a group. Eventually, they traveled together. They got to know each other at a much different level through being friends first. Charlotte notes, "I could try him on as a partner from the beginning. I could see different sides of him. It gave each of us a lens to look through to see different sides of each other. We have been through a lot together as friends. We have both focused on parenting. We share a goal of being the best parent you can, not getting sidetracked with personal distraction which could create instability in childhood."

Steve has been married before too. Charlotte and Steve both have sons the same age. They are both willing to accept responsibility for what happened to break down the relationship during their marriages. They are willing to ask the hard questions such as, what role did you play to create whatever insecurity began to break down the relationship? They accept that it is important to not point fingers. The relationship did not break down because of one event. Charlotte and Steve can both ask, "What did I bring to this equation? How will I be in the present?"

Charlotte is willing to ask the hard questions. "Where do insecurities come from?" She acknowledges we have to talk to our inner child and nurture her needs so you don't carry insecurities into the next relationship.'

Charlotte cites character as the quality that is most attractive to her. "That we were friends for so long allowed me to see the kind of character he brought to the relationship. He was the kind of man who could love and be loyal; that character was enormously attractive. Every blessing has a burden; it's not one sided. He expects the same thing in return. Forgiveness and grace are qualities of character that made him attractive. Learning to trust someone's character becomes difficult after divorce. There is a level of vulnerability when you love. Steve needs to be cared for in the same way."

According to Charlotte, more experience has brought her an awareness of a different kind of love. "We love each other the best we can, but showing up is a different level of love. I can see it differently now. Young love produces excitement about the kind of future you can have together. But coming into relationship later, you're looking for a companion to walk through life with. You're seeking day-to-day support, showing up for the other person. Separate but connected is a skill to learn in all relationships. It is a valuable insight to learn how to be truly connected but okay to be separate. Knowing that is a part of our relationship that gives me peace. It is a good place to be."

One of the things Charlotte and Steve are cognizant of is that second and third marriages divorce at a higher rate. Trying to be with other people's children and the relationships you have within that framework can be challenging. Charlotte acknowledges, "The complexity of that is high risk. I could be allowing another person to destroy my relationship with my child or his relationship with himself. It's too risky at present. Statistically, it doesn't work."

For those reasons, Charlotte and Steve have put marriage plans on hold. "I want to be married again, but in God's time. We are trying to allow that to happen with the goals that each of us has for raising our children. Letting God direct us is far better than me trying to contrive or manipulate what I want. Another lesson of self-discovery involves trying not to force things to happen because of things you think you want. Historically, through my life, looking at times God has shown up is wonderful. Documenting, in my mind, this way of letting things happen rather than forcing or grasping is helpful. You need to trust in that."

Charlotte acknowledges being patient is hard. "Hormones and lust can cloud what you think you want. When I allow God to show me what I need, it all comes together. It helps to see how this happened and then that happens. Everything is working together for my good is an important concept to note. What He is showing me today is important. Whether wholeness comes is circumstantial. Sometimes insecurity rears its ugly head. Sometimes I just need my partner to be on my side. It is a process. I'm probably stronger than I've ever been."

Charlotte and Steve have two goals that inform their relationship. Make time for fun and keep it simple. Take time out to play. Do everything with the best of intentions.

CHAPTER 13
Transformation

<u>Both Sides Now</u>
The Nancy Sharp Story

The themes of "The Journey Within: Living After Loss" include the loss itself, pain, struggle, grief, courage, resilience, and finally renewal. All are exemplified in the story of Nancy Sharp, writer and speechwriter. In her bestseller, <u>Both Sides Now</u>, Nancy chronicles her own journey. When I read it, I knew it would be the perfect last story for my book with a positive ending after very difficult life experiences.

Both Sides Now is Nancy Sharp's personal story of love and loss, courage, resilience, and healing. Even though it is told through her lens, the author wanted her story to be a bridge for others, to share and reflect their own experiences of loss. "I chose the title not as a song of mourning, but as a frame to hold all of life. I wanted the reader to reflect on his/her own experience."

Nancy knows love and loss. Married very young, their idyllic life was shattered when Brett was diagnosed with a pediatric brain tumor. His promising career at Time Warner was just beginning. Nancy, meanwhile, was doing purposeful work with UNICEF USA. Brett's diagnosis was not part of their life plans. Not letting your world define you is something Nancy feels strongly about. "We get to write our own story; we must be the authors of our story."

Courageously, they decided to go forward anyway with plans for the family they desired. After lengthy treatment, Brett's cancer seemed to be in remission. The treatment was shrinking the tumor. They would proceed. Nancy explained, "No one ever said the words, 'he is cured.'

It's just that life was happening all around us and we so wanted the future we always dreamed of having that we made this our narrative. It was the most life-affirming thing we could do."

Nancy decided to trust the process, believing in her body's ability to conceive through in vitro. Only weeks after learning they were pregnant, the doctor gave them the astounding news that he saw two heartbeats.

All was not peaceful during this time of waiting. Nancy reported having pregnant anxiety dreams. Her default position was a simple, calming mantra. She describes, "I was not sustained by faith during this time. That came later."

Nancy reported trying to bargain with God suggesting that if the cancer had to come back, might it wait until the twins were fully grown?

When she was only thirty weeks pregnant, Nancy woke up one spring morning to heavy spotting. She and Brett raced off to the hospital but because her cervix was still fully closed, the couple's OBGYN discharged them. There was no real way to know that hours later she would feel a gush of water. The babies were to be born that day.

A vaginal birth followed. Rebecca weighed two and a half pounds. Casey was bigger. He weighed three pounds two ounces.

Late that afternoon, Brett's cell phone rang. His neuro-oncologist had an urgent message. The "routine" MRI he'd taken a few days prior was back and this time the scan showed a tumor in his brain and one in his spine. This is the pivotal moment in Nancy's stunning story of love and loss. There was the dichotomy of new life and the threat of death all on the same day. This was too cruel to contemplate. They were unraveled. They marshaled their courage and just moved from day to day. This is the way Nancy describes the time period after the babies were born. "I just rose up. You do what is in front of you. I had newborn babies."

Brett was always focused on his family's well-being and staying on the job. It seemed his life and death struggle took a back seat to these goals. He would fight it with aggressive treatment because of these priorities. He would put all his energy and focus into living.

At some point, a final MRI was done revealing the dreaded news that the cancer had spread throughout Brett's brain in chunks of tumor. Mini seizures began to eat away at his cognition. Home hospice care was arranged when the twins were only thirty-two months old. The hospice aides kept reminding Nancy that dignity and self-preservation were vital. That things were dire didn't describe the destruction. But still, Nancy reports she wanted more time. Even so, when the end came, Nancy could let him go.

One of the most difficult things Nancy went through in the aftermath of Brett's death was widowhood. She says being seen as a widow created pain for her. "I wore widowhood like a scarlet letter across my forehead. It was a terrible stigma I created for myself. I felt defined by it, telling people I was a widow before I would tell them I was a mother or writer. It was tragedy upon tragedy that during this time I was punishing myself in some way. I couldn't see clearly until I was ready to lift that veil."

Nancy recalls, "I lost a whole decade. I lost my entire 30's to caregiving and mourning. It wasn't until I was in my mid-forties that I began to write 'Both Sides Now' in earnest. I had finally gained the perspective to be able to distill and integrate all those experiences into the fabric of my life today."

As young as the twins were in the aftermath of losing their father, they found ways to express their feelings. Nancy remembers, "My son was very perceptive, very spiritual, and very intuitive. He found his voice in ways that were hard to understand. I don't know where that comes from. It was just some kind of spiritual gift, quite frankly. He would say profound things to me, putting his hand on my face for comfort."

During this time, there was a social worker helping the twins to define what was happening. They needed to deal with what happened in very concrete terms.

In the months after Brett's death, Nancy had to face the inevitable. She noted, "There was no life insurance. We had practical considerations, financial considerations." So she began to consider a move away from New York City. The fact that their apartment had increased in value made it financially possible to relocate. That's how she wound up moving to Colorado in 2006.

Nancy insists the courage to pick up and move can be defined in all kinds of ways. "Boldness is the ability to move forward. You don't have to move across the country to be bold. You just need the courage to see beyond and to look beyond what is defining you."

Nancy says two things have to happen in order to be really bold. "The first is you have to be smart enough to realize you're really stuck. Then you have to trust in an expanded view of your world. You have to develop a perspective about your circumstances. You have to realize that you have opportunities. Then, before you know it, you're on your way. The most important thing is to just keep stepping forward, moving from one step to the next. Then you prove something to yourself as you move forward.

Moving away from New York City allowed Nancy to heal. She needed to leave the illness and death that had shadowed her in Manhattan and embrace Denver's sunshine and big sky.

Nancy recalls, "In January, 2007, I found myself sitting at the breakfast table alone. I was feeling a little bit lackluster. I was reading a newspaper column about a TV news anchor who'd also been widowed, and he was being featured as one of Denver's most eligible singles. It ignited something within me. I decided to send this Steve Saunders an email. " Nancy observes that never in a million years did she think she'd actually marry Steve. That's the stuff of Hollywood! Nancy notes, "I reached out to Steve for one reason only: I needed to assert myself in life." Steve didn't email her back the first time. A couple of weeks passed before she decided to try again. This time, he responded right away. He was very apologetic...and overwhelmed. Even though he was in the public eye, he was very shy. It had been four years since his wife died.

Nancy asserts she doesn't necessarily think things are meant to be. She acknowledges if she hadn't moved to Colorado, she would never have met Steve, but she doesn't believe that things are preordained. Brett's illness is a case in point. According to Nancy, "There is no rationale for why healthy, young people get terrible diseases. Sometimes shitty things happen, and you know what? There's no rhyme or reason. You just go forward. Nancy was always clear that she wanted to use her experience in a way that could benefit others. That's what motivated her to write *Both Sides Now*. "I didn't see writing my story as a risk. I knew that I had a unique way of rending my story and helping people understand the sometimes dueling realities of life and death. "

Through all of Nancy's experiences, she has learned the importance of being quiet. "We need moments to reflect and make sense of life. I am really conscious of that today. My life is intentionally quieter now."

Nancy's ongoing life reflects the cumulative awareness she has gained from losing Brett and marrying another widower. "In our present lives, we find times to honor Steve's wife, Pam, and Brett. We do it as a family and sometimes just with our respective children. We certainly reflect on Brett and Pam at holidays, birthdays, and rites of passage, but also in subtler, moments when memories rise to the surface that we want to share."

The universal appeal of Nancy's story becomes apparent as she meets people all over the country. "A lot of people approach me who have experienced loss and hurt and adversity of all kinds. You can't be part of the human experience without loss. It affects everybody: the young, a lot of seniors, men, women, people in rural communities, big cities and global locales. Here's the thing…just as loss is universal, so too, is hope. You must find ways to integrate your losses so that you can get back to living.

The transformation that has taken place in Nancy's life mirrors my own. People come into our lives when we're ready for them. Sometimes we have to move on from the life we planned so the life that is planned for us can come forth. Writing the book feels like what I was supposed to do. The result has been my own transformation.

CHAPTER 14
Loss and Grief

When I thought about what I have learned from the generous sharing I have experienced, I was struck by how much loss had been experienced by the people I had met and interviewed. I turned to my expert on loss, my sister Grace Harlow Klein, Ph.D. who has written about loss and grief and is a psychotherapist in the Center for Human Encouragement. She wrote, "Divorce or death of a partner begins a process of loss and grief. The feelings and experiences that emerge are unique to each individual, according to the nature of the relationship, the length and depth of the connection one had with that person. Even relief from a negative relationship is still a complex experience accompanied by guilt and self-questioning and self-blame as things are often clearer in hindsight. "Why didn't I …" "I should have…" "Why did I ever…" is a part of regret which may be universal in the process of grief.

Every aspect of a person's life is changed in the loss of a significant relationship. The wonderful things that brought joy are now mourned. The loss of identity, friendships, financial stability and home can all be affected by both death and divorce. When children are involved, there are many challenges because the children are experiencing their own losses. Parenting becomes much more difficult as is evident in Nancy Sharp's story with her twins..

Another aspect prominent in some of the stories is the issue of care-giving which many persons experienced with spouses or parents and spouses before death occurred. Care-giving, even when done lovingly out of the richness of a relationship, is still debilitating. It takes over one's life, energy, thoughts and emotions. It takes even longer to restore one's health after the end of caregiving. In fact, some caregivers do not survive the process and die before the one they cared for. The sense of oneself must be restored before a new relationship can be successful – as is apparent in some of the stories.

"How long does it take?" is a frequent question by those in the grip of grief? It takes as long as it takes – if one works at the feelings of grief and loss. Time does not heal all wounds but it takes time to work with the losses. Susan Gantz, whose husband died suddenly and tragically wrote, "The only thing I know for sure out of this experience of loss is that time helps, connections with people, animals and nature help. And for me, art has offered a means of relief I don't really understand.

The pain involved in loss and grief is not under one's control. It just is – and the brain shuts down, creating a sense of deadness, confusion, not feeling like oneself. Creating a language for the feelings of grief and loss is essential, along with the awareness of the physical experiences within ones' body.

Grief is also an active process of one step after another – first dealing with what has to be done, gradually giving way to choices about the life we create in the empty space. As one emerges from the pain, one begins to feel "like myself again," a self forever changed by the experiences of the life one had and by the loss of it. It is only in the Dolores Story and somewhat in Nancy Sharp's that there is evidence of cultural support for this process of grief – a timeframe, a set of activities, active participation by others with the bereaved one.

Interestingly, in the open space which I called The Space Between in my book, Transition, one may have access to all of the good feelings and memories of the person who is no longer there, integrating them into an overall sense of one's life.

At its core, one has to let in, "I am alone" — with all of the fear, confusion and other feelings that accompany it. For many, it is the first time one has lived alone, going from childhood home to marriage, creating uneasiness in the space of aloneness. Old feelings from infancy and childhood may emerge in this process, feelings of abandonment, not being cared for. It is an existential crisis for in reality each of us is alone in our own skin. Coming to terms with that reality, becoming comfortable with oneself is freeing — the doors opening to possibilities to create our own world with whatever challenges accompany that.

In my life, I have experienced times of intense loss beginning with the tragic death of my five year old sister when I was fourteen. I have struggled with each of these losses with sadness, grief and despair at times. But as I look back, I see that my experience in each loss led me to a new time of growth — which brought great happiness and purpose in my life.

That process is happening once again in the aftermath of the death of my much loved husband whom I cared for at home with the amazing help of others. My books, A Bridge of Returning, Loss, and Transition reflect my experiences. Each of them combines prose poetry, photography and art I created in those losses. Kaleidoscope: My Changing World will soon be out, the conclusion of writing that began eighteen years ago at a time of significant loss in my world of work.

In the stories recorded by Coralie Harlow Robertson from her interviews, the complexities of loss are evident in most, if not all, of the stories. One can sense who has done the work of grief, who not. Only three stories included a reference to the use of psychotherapy or bereavement help in their process. But it is a very powerful facilitator of the process of grief to have someone to talk with as one navigates this very complex path or to share with members of a bereavement group

Coralie experienced the process of going inward as she shares in her book – the process she named, <u>The Journey Within: Living After Loss</u> and then reached out to others who shared their stories with her."

CHAPTER 15
What I Learned

It was only after reading <u>Both Sides Now</u>, Nancy Sharp's story of love and loss, that I began to realize it had all the components of my own journey within. There were similar themes of loss, struggle, resilience and transformation. It was only in retrospect that I began to recognize a similar pattern in interviews. Coincidence or chance encounter would lead me to just the right story or person. I have learned to trust the process.

One of the unexpected benefits of my own journey within was finding my voice. The time came in my relationship with Will that I was able to sit down with him and put a voice to my feelings. I shared with him once more all the wonderful things I appreciated about him. For perhaps the first time, I was also able to express what I didn't appreciate. It was a very emotional time for both of us. Will was able to express that he was never unaware of the pain I was going through. He said, "Coralie, it is difficult to conceive that much of our relationship was not a happy time for either one of us." We both agreed we wanted to continue the deep friendship we had shared. We parted on very good terms that day. I released something and recognized how healing it had been.

Fate intervened in my life at this point. The very next day, I met Paul. There was a spark between us from the outset. Paul is a writer also. We exchanged emails and phone numbers. Paul wanted to share some of his book with me. Needless to say, we discovered a lot to talk about. We both have been willing to put ourselves "out there" in very honest communication. It appears we might be developing a relationship, possibly the kind of relationship we both desire.

The journey within after loss has become my destination. While following the lessons and stories of relationships offered during the interviews, it became clear to me that this journey should not be avoided if wholeness is your goal. I have come to regard pain and difficulty as a gift. My chances of a successful, long-term relationship are greater now than when I was looking to the relationship to fill a void. Going within is the first rule of healing after loss. Leaning on my spiritual strength, I am learning to be whole on my own.

I have learned that loss is an inevitable part of being human. None of us escapes. Whether your loss involves the death of a partner or divorce, resulting in the loss of a relationship you had counted on going the distance, it hurts. Additionally, the loss itself may result in "magical thinking" where our thought processes cannot be relied on for a while. It is no time to be making large decisions about our life or relationships. It takes time. We struggle. We all will experience loneliness at times.

Through my interviews resulting in stories about people experiencing loss, I have learned that going through "The Journey Within" can be a healing process. I began to note a correlation in the stories of people involved in a relationship. If they engaged in the journey within prior to or during the course of the relationship, there were more successes. If not, the relationship often failed at some point.

I have learned that there is hope. It is woven into the fabric of the stories. Serial relationships are occurring more often in our population of seniors still living vigorous lives.

I have learned that living your life with intention can be healing. I made a choice to actively participate in the process of building the next chapter of my life. Often, true growth seems to be accompanied by struggle, at least that has been my experience. There is reason to be optimistic. Little did I know when I began, that this journey within would wake up a whole segment of myself.

Bibliography

Cloud, Henry. and Townsend, John. *Boundaries in Dating: How Healthy Choices Grow Healthy Relationships*. Grand Rapids: Zondervan, 2000. Print.

Emanuel, Ezekiel J. "Sex and the Single Senior." *nytimes.com*. The New York Times Company. 18 January 2014. Web. 15 March 2016.

Hellmich, Nanci. "Feeling Lonely? It May Increase Risk of Early Death." *usatoday.com*. Gannett, 17 February 2014. Web. 3 January 2016.

Starkey, Scott. "Can You Really Die of a Broken Heart?" *startribune.com*. Star Tribune, 4 June 2014. Web. 10 February 2016.

Sun, Key Ph.D. *"Why Online Dating is a Poor Way to Find Love." The Justice and Responsibility League*. Psychology Today. 29 July 2010. Web. 2 March 2016.

About the Author

When Coralie Harlow Robertson's husband of fifty-four years passed away, she never imagined that it would be the catalyst for her first published book. As she picked up the pieces of grief and began building the next chapter of her life, <u>The Journey Within: Living After Loss</u> began taking shape. Not only is her book a beacon of hope for those who are exploring the options of relationships after loss, becoming an author is an opportunity for her to model that it is never too late to try something new to her four children, six grandchildren and five great-grandchildren. As a retired teacher and a current mentor to young people at The Prodigy Leadership Academy, being a stellar example of compassion and humanity is an important ideal that Coralie strives for daily.

Author photograph by John Mark